Sweet Track to Glastonbury

NEW ASPECTS OF ANTIQUITY

General Editor: COLIN RENFREW

Consulting Editor for the Americas: JEREMY A. SABLOFF

BRYONY AND JOHN COLES

Sweet Track to Glastonbury

The Somerset Levels in Prehistory

with 146 illustrations, 16 in color

THAMES AND HUDSON

For Jack Coles and Jean Orme
who have made all things possible

Frontispiece: A reconstruction of the Glastonbury Lake Village.
Drawn by R. Walker.

Drawings by Sue Rouillard, unless otherwise stated in the captions.

First published in the United States in 1986 by
Thames and Hudson Inc., 500 Fifth Avenue,
New York, New York 10110

Library of Congress Catalog Card Number 85-51949

Printed and bound in Great Britain

Contents

All the prehistoric dates quoted in this book are derived from radiocarbon assay, and are given here in radiocarbon years bc. The problems of calibration to calendar years are touched on in chapter 4. At present, the interpretation of the prehistory of the Levels is not significantly affected by calibration. Where we have used calendar dates, for historical references, we have quoted them as BC or AD.

General Editor's foreword

Preservation is the key to archaeology: the survival, that is, of the physical remains of the past down to our own time. This is what is so altogether remarkable about the Somerset Levels. The peat of the wetlands has highly effective preservative properties, so that wood and plant remains are admirably preserved (although bone and shell rapidly decay in that acid environment). Such preservation has allowed a whole new dimension of life in prehistoric Britain to be brought to light in the systematic researches into the Somerset Levels which are described here.

Traces of woodworking are in general very rare until the Late Saxon period in this country, and for the prehistoric period exceedingly so. The indications of skilled woodworking found in the great prehistoric trackways which have been revealed by the Somerset Levels Project, as well as the various wooden artifacts – not least the now-famous Neolithic 'God-Dolly' – throw a brilliant shaft of light upon an otherwise obscure area of our knowledge.

The detailed study of the wood from the trackways, undertaken by specialists, has led to a greatly increased understanding of tree-husbandry practices, that is to say of coppicing, which adds an important new dimension to our picture of man's relationship with the landscape at this early time. Indeed the whole thrust of this book is towards the deeper understanding of the human place within the natural environment, and of their mutual interactions. The feeling which the authors have for the flat yet varied Somerset landscape comes over on every page.

The Somerset Levels Project was the first in this country to tackle in a systematic way one of our most important but fast dwindling archaeological resources: the wetlands. Like the fens of East Anglia, the Somerset Levels are being drained at a rapid pace, and the damp conditions that have preserved so much archaeological information in the past are fast disappearing. As this book so well brings out, we are losing not only an important part of our natural environment in Britain, but also the vast potential for archaeological research which the wetlands possess. The Project was the first to perceive the full scale of this threat, and its lead has now been followed in the East Anglian fens. The story of its origins and development into a remarkable and pioneering piece of rescue archaeology is told here.

It had its earlier beginnings in the work of Bulleid and Gray at the famous Iron Age lake village of Glastonbury, excavated in the early years of this century. The same H. St. George Gray, who had served in his youth as an assistant to General Pitt Rivers, the great pioneer of systematic excavation in this country, was still to be found in his eighties, excavating in the 1950s at the lake village of Meare. There, as a schoolboy in about 1952, I had the privilege of meeting him, and I value the recollection of this dedicated old man still working at Meare so many years after his training with Pitt Rivers. The work at the lake villages of Glastonbury and Meare revealed more clearly than anywhere else a full picture of life in Iron Age Britain, and it is indeed one of the merits of the work of Bryony and John Coles that they are preparing for final publication the findings of Gray in his later excavations at Meare. One of the absorbing features of this book is their discussion of the various interpretations of the findings at Glastonbury and Meare which have been made by such energetic and ingenious later scholars as E. Tratman and D. L. Clarke. The broader environmental perspective of this more recent work has much to offer when brought to bear on these earlier interpretations.

The most exciting part of the story, however, is undoubtedly the detective work and the sustained and persistent research which led to the recognition and investigation of the prehistoric trackways, culminating in the discovery of the 'oldest road in the world', the Neolithic Sweet Track. The story of its discovery, excavation ('No feet on peat') and its conservation is indeed a fascinating one.

There are many insights here into prehistoric life and into modern archaeology. They are presented with a deep sympathy for the landscape and for the traditional life of the Somerset Levels, both of which are now subject to such drastic change that their survival is currently in doubt.

Colin Renfrew

1 Man and landscape

As in summer time it may really be termed a summer-country so no less may it in the winter season be called a winter-country; so wet, moist and marshy it is for the most part; which makes it very troublesome to travellers.

(W. Camden 1607)

A land of green meadows, watery rhynes, and black peatfields, its flatness relieved only by stubby willows and grazing cows, the Somerset Levels seem timeless and unchanging to the visitor. Nothing could be further from the truth, for the story of this land is one of evolution and change, and of man's struggle to master its unrelenting floods. In this book we hope to show how landscape, drainage, vegetation, animals and the pattern of human settlement have evolved through the centuries, their alterations interacting to produce a sequence of events that we can sometimes only glimpse, and sometimes comprehend more fully when the evidence is abundant. plate I plate II

In the chapters that follow, we shall be largely concerned with the changing pattern of human life in the Levels from 4000 bc to the Roman Conquest, as well as with the nature of the evidence and our methods of study. It will be immediately apparent that the present archaeology of the Levels, and its past history, has been dominated by water, and it is appropriate to examine why this is so.

The Levels may be seen as a broad trough, edged by the hills of the Mendips to the north and the Quantocks to the south, blocked by the gently rising hinterland of Somerset to the east and wide open to the sea on the west. Every rise and fall of sea-level in Pleistocene and recent times has affected this low-lying area, which has been transformed many a time from the shallow bay of a high sea-level to freshwater marshes as the sea retreated. Extreme falls of sea-level, such as occurred during the latter part of the last glaciation when ice-sheets locked up vast masses of water, placed the region sufficiently beyond the influence of salt water and tides for a dry, grassy plain to develop. But such a dry state was exceptional, and since the end of the last ice-age some ten thousand years ago, the region has varied merely in its degree of excess water. This is not only due to the proximity of the sea; the basin of the Levels collects water from a particularly wide catchment area where rainfall is high, and the fall to sea-level is so slight that inflow can easily surpass outflow. The problems are compounded by high tides surging up the Bristol Channel. fig. 1 plate 1

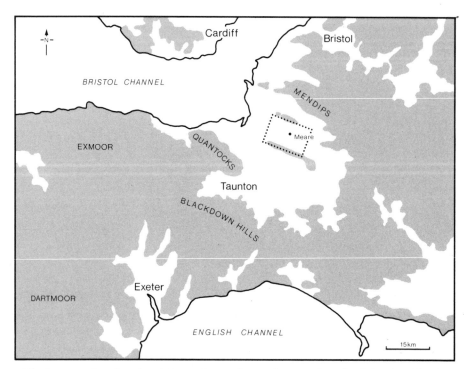

1 The Somerset Levels, a low-lying region in the south-west of England, bordered by the Bristol Channel and the Mendip, Quantock and Blackdown Hills. The rectangle indicates the area of intensive archaeological work shown in greater detail in subsequent maps.

From the time of the first written records of the Levels, the annual winter floods have been singled out as their outstanding feature, exerting control over the whole history and evolution of the region. In 1607, a particularly disastrous period of rainfall brought floodwaters to the foot of Glastonbury Tor (22 km inland): 'In a short tyme did whole villages stand like islands, compassed round with Waters, and in a short tyme were these islands undiscoverable, and no where to be found. The tops of trees and houses onely appeared, especially there where the Country lay lowe, as if at the beginning of the world townes had been builte in the bottome of the Sea, and that people had plaide the husbandmen under the Waters.' The peatlands of the Brue valley lay under 3–4 m of water, and these floods were almost matched in succeeding centuries; in 1794, the Tor was again reached by floodwaters, and again in 1800, 1853, and 1872–73 when 107 square miles were under water from October to March: 'the floods though excessive were not altogether exceptional'. In 1936, most of the Brue valley was under water, and in 1960 a very wet October and November led to eighty-six consecutive days of floods. Since the mid-1960s, our sites have often been inundated by heavy rain, and during one or two summer seasons, the sites lay under water and invisible as the fields around were also submerged. It is only in recent decades that the problems of winter

fig. 2

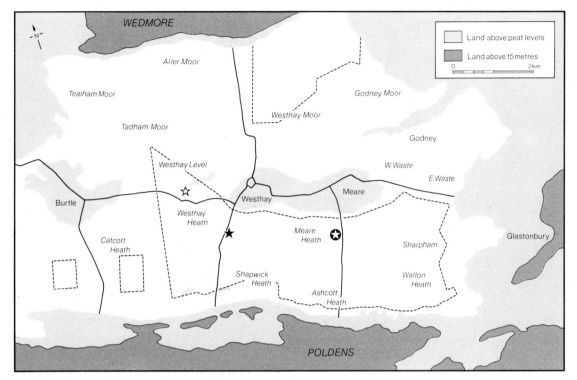

⊛ Project HQ
★ Museum
☆ Abbot's Way
  Reconstruction

2 *The Brue valley, centre of the peat-cutting industry and focus of the work of the Somerset Levels Project. Heath, waste and moor are traditional terms for the common peatlands. The dashed line marks the areas of intensive peat-cutting.*

flooding have been largely overcome, to the detriment of the Levels as a natural wetland, but to the benefit of many an inhabitant, whether farmer or peat-cutter.

Persistent waterlogging of the lowland has led to the formation over time of great deposits of peat. This does not occur in all wetlands, but in Somerset the interplay of local conditions allowed vegetation to grow almost without interruption, whilst the waterlogging was yet frequent enough and deep enough to hinder the decay of dead plant material. Through the centuries, plate 2 roots and rhizomes, leaves and stems, matted sedges and hummocks of moss accumulated in varying stages of partial decomposition until layers of peat several metres in depth covered the wetland area. As the layers built up, the surface was raised, providing slightly less wet conditions for plant growth, only to be flooded anew from time to time as the general water-table itself fluctuated. The detailed history of vegetational change in the Levels is complex, due to the subtle interplay of water-levels, nutrients and surface conditions, but the broad outline of change from about 4000 bc to about ad 400 is now well-established.

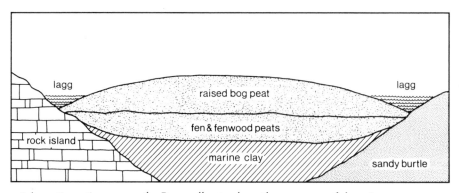

3 Schematic section across the Brue valley to show the sequence of deposits.

fig. 3

plate III

plate IV

Early in the fourth millennium bc all the low-lying land to the east of the Bristol Channel was under sea water. The Channel itself was wider and deeper than it is now, present-day ridges and hills such as Brent Knoll stood out as islands in the tidal waters, and Glastonbury Tor was situated at the end of a long thin peninsula. Everywhere the sea reached, a layer of blue-grey marine clay was deposited. By 3600 bc the sea had begun to retreat, and in the easternmost reaches, reeds colonized the brackish waters. By 3000 bc the Levels were a sea of reed and sedge cut by sluggish, meandering drainage channels, and wherever enough dead plant matter had accumulated, water-tolerant trees such as willow and birch became established. Gradually the trees encroached on the reeds and swathes of fenwood spread across the wetland. Within a few centuries they too had raised the growing surface to the point where new plant communities became established, this time the mosses, cotton-grass and heather of a raised bog which drew largely on rainwater as the accumulated peat had now built up beyond the ground water-level. From time to time floodwaters overtook the bog, and plant life adapted, but large tracts of raised bog appear to have flourished until peat-growth ceased in the early centuries AD.

Waterlogging and the survival of the evidence

Throughout this long sequence of waterlogging and peat formation, anything caught in the tangled mass of vegetation on the growing surface was rapidly buried in dead, wet plant matter, and it too remained wet thereafter. Waterlogging excludes oxygen and delays bacterial and fungal decay; under these conditions, organic material has a good chance of survival, not perhaps unaltered but in a far more complete state than when conditions are dry or fluctuating. It is for this reason that, whereas on most archaeological sites archery is represented by flint arrowheads alone, in the Levels fragments of arrowshaft and a number of bows have also survived.

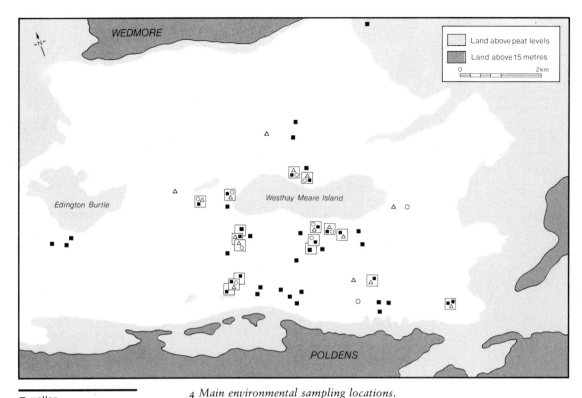

4 *Main environmental sampling locations.*

■ pollen
△ plant macrofossils
○ beetles

The preservation of organic material depends too on other aspects of ground conditions, such as the acidity of the deposits. In much of the Levels, local conditions favour the survival of plant remains, such as wood, but with the exception of one category (see below) animal remains are known only from sites where the acidity of the peat has been counteracted by localized deposits of clay or a heavy inwash of minerals from adjacent slopes. Such conditions exist for the Iron Age settlement sites of Glastonbury and Meare, where bone has survived in great quantity (see chapter 7), but elsewhere traces of birds and mammals are very faint.

It is the survival of plant materials which lends such richness to the archaeology of the Levels, and the best-known and most dramatic of these is the survival of wood, from the intimate scale of personal artifacts such as bowls, paddles or pins, to the massive wooden platforms and trackways built from thousands of individual components. Often, the wood survives as an object or a structure quite unknown from dryland sites, such as a wooden fork or a hurdle pathway. The wealth of evidence provided by the wood will be immediately apparent from the illustrations throughout this book, and the framework for the chronological unfolding of man's presence in the Levels is wood, not stone or metal.

But the looming presence of great planks and ingenious hurdles must not blind us to the contribution made by other categories of plant material. Perhaps the most significant of these is pollen, well-stratified in the peat and representing the changing vegetation of the surrounding dryland as well as that of the marsh. Pollen provides the environmental context for man's activities in the region, particularly that of the dryland in terms of forested or open land and the first tenuous traces of agriculture. The more localized wetland context is known of course not only from the pollen, but also from the macroscopic plants of the peat.

The one category of animal evidence that survives well in wet acid peat is the chitin of insect exoskeletons. Beetles are well-represented, especially by wing-cases, and can be identified to species; knowledge of their present habitats leads to very detailed reconstruction of past conditions. Insect evidence complements pollen and plant macro-studies for both wetland and dryland contexts, and may include indicators of agriculture.

fig. 4

Archaeology is not only a matter of artifacts, and it has always been our aim, and that of several of our predecessors in the Levels, to exploit to the full the range of environmental evidence that accompanies, engulfs and sometimes is one and the same as the organic archaeological material from the peat. The closeness of the links is evident in such aspects as the development of tree-ring analyses and the study of woodland composition and woodland management on the slopes around the marshes. All of the evidence, whether directly associated with human activity or whether relatively independent, has a bearing on our study of human occupation of the region, because the context inevitably affects patterns of settlements and of exploitation.

Peat-cutting

Waterlogging preserves the evidence, cushioned in and forming part of the peat which characterizes the Levels. Peat-cutting, another feature typical of the region, both destroys the evidence and makes it available for study. Without cutting, there is no knowing what lies buried in the peat, for there are no surface indications of sites. Aerial photographs have never revealed buried trackways. With cutting, the evidence is physically removed, or exposed to destructive processes, but the cutting provides the one chance to discover, observe, and study the record preserved in the peat. It is therefore relevant to look briefly at the history of peat-cutting in the region, and to consider how it may have affected the archaeological record.

Although the earlier historic records are patchy, and do not always refer directly to peat-cutting, there is enough information from diverse sources to suggest regular cutting for fuel during the course of perhaps 1500 years. The earliest evidence is archaeological: a Romano-British salt-making mound where peat-ash shows the fuel used in the evaporation process. Some centuries later, a Saxon boundary charter uses moors as reference points and includes moors within an estate, suggesting that they were valued land, though whether for peat or for other resources we cannot be sure. Domesday entries refer to moors, and ecclesiastical documents dating from the centuries between Domesday and the Dissolution of the Monasteries in 1535 contain many references to moors and turbaries and make specific mention of the cutting of peat. The most vivid picture comes from the thirteenth century when rivalry between the Bishop of Bath and Wells and the Abbot of Glastonbury was running high (as it so often was). One year, piqued by the Bishop, the Abbot ordered large-scale cutting of peat from the moors south of Meare, and there was removed 'all the peat of that great moor so that for ten years or more, every hearth in Glastonbury was plentifully supplied.'

This incident suggests that peat was a regular fuel at the time, if not perhaps always so abundant. Its household use for heat and cooking must have exposed and destroyed much archaeological evidence over the centuries, and who knows what was lost in the Abbot's great operation. It is obvious, however, that medieval cutting removed the top layers of the peat, which were the most recently formed and which contained evidence from the post-Roman period. Due to high water-tables and the limitations of pre-industrial technology, it is highly unlikely that medieval peat-cutters penetrated far into the prehistoric levels.

However, by the nineteenth century, intensive cutting was exposing and destroying prehistoric deposits in a few, probably fairly restricted areas. We know where this was happening with the recorded discovery of the Neolithic Abbot's Way in about 1834, but many nineteenth-century finds of bronze tools, weapons and ornaments have no provenance other than 'turbaries west of Glastonbury'. Even the famous Edington Burtle hoard has no precise location (see pp. 135–6).

If nineteenth-century cutters were able in a few places to reach down to Neolithic levels, it was largely because of the cumulative effect of several centuries of drainage, and subsequent efforts have made it possible to extract peat to the lowest levels of the fourth millennium bc. Until the mid-twentieth century, the techniques of cutting required little other than muscle-power, to   plate 3
cut and lift and stack and turn the blocks of peat, and then to cart them to the   plate 4
hearths where they were burnt. During the 1950s, some rapid changes set in,
cutting became mechanized and the peat was increasingly sold for fertilizer or   plate VI
horticultural growing-medium rather than fuel. Mechanization and ever-
improving drainage have greatly accelerated the rate of extraction, together
with the exposure and removal or decay of archaeological evidence. It has been   plate 5
our good fortune to work in the Levels at a time when archaeological field-
work was urgently required and highly rewarding.

Since all of the peat-cutting in the Levels began with the raised bog peats, which are best both for burning and for the provision of fertilizers, the archaeological record that has emerged is to a great extent confined to those areas where raised bogs existed. In the southern part of the Levels, on Sedgemoor, there is very little raised bog peat and cutting has never been a feature of this large area. Thus most of our record comes from the Brue valley, although the Sedgemoor finds are noted at intervals in this book.

Chronological outline

The discoveries, and the studies, have been such that we can draw a firm outline of prehistory in the Levels, set in the context of environmental change. The sequence of events is summarized in fig. 5 but starts a little earlier than the initiation of peat growth, with Mesolithic foragers on the sandy islands (known locally as burtles) that dot the low-lying landscape. Their presence is known only from the flints they left behind, a 'dryland' archaeology, and it is not certain if they were present when the Levels were covered by the sea and the burtles were truly islands, reached by boat, or if the foragers crossed marshland to reach the drier ground. The flints include both early and late Mesolithic types, so use of the landscape or seascape in varied conditions is possible but not proven. As the Mesolithic record is at present a dryland one, the foragers have figured little in our work; we remain alert, however, to the possibility of tracing their presence in the earlier post-glacial peats that underlie the marine clay, and in the very lowest levels of the fourth-millennium deposits.

Colour plates (pages 17, 18)

I View of the Somerset Levels, with the edge of the Polden Hills on the right, meadows and grazing land, and dark peatfields in the distance. One of the small sand islands, called burtles, is visible just left of centre.

II A traditional scene in the Levels, with pollard willows edging the rhyne, grazing cows and rain clouds gathering.

III Fen woodland in the Shapwick Heath Nature Reserve, with lush vegetation growing on the wet peat. Beneath the surface in this area lies the unexcavated Sweet Track.

IV Cotton-grass on a wet surface of a former raised bog, now partly cut-away and poorly drained. *Sphagnum* moss, some rush and small birch, willow and even oak have also colonized.

I

II

III IV

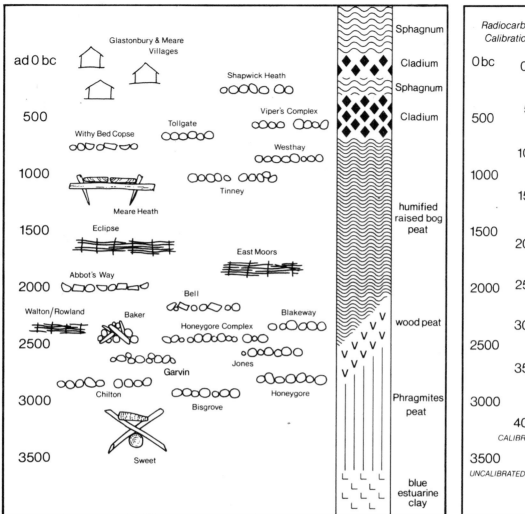

ad 0 bc		Sphagnum
	Glastonbury & Meare Villages	Cladium
		Sphagmum
500	Shapwick Heath	
	Viper's Complex	Cladium
	Tollgate	
	Withy Bed Copse	
1000	Westhay	
	Tinney	
	Meare Heath	humified raised bog peat
1500	Eclipse	
	East Moors	
2000	Abbot's Way	
	Bell	
	Walton/Rowland Baker Blakeway	wood peat
2500	Honeygore Complex	
	Jones	
	Garvin	
3000	Chilton Honeygore	Phragmites peat
	Bisgrove	
3500	Sweet	blue estuarine clay

Radiocarbon Calibration	
0 bc	0 BC
	500
500	1000
1000	1500
1500	2000
2000	2500
	3000
2500	3500
3000	4000
	CALIBRATED
3500	UNCALIBRATED

5 *Diagrammatic representation of the sequence of structures and changing peat deposits in the Levels, from 3500 bc to the end of the prehistoric period, with calibration chart.*

The wetland environmental record of the Levels begins in the earlier fourth millennium bc, with deciduous forest on the dryland and sedge and reed flourishing in the wet areas left by the retreating sea. A few centuries later, the first sign of people living in the marshes appears: at much the same time as our first evidence for farmers in Britain. The evidence is dramatic: the long and massive Sweet Track (chapter 3) built entirely of wood and, for archaeologist and environmentalist alike, a treasure-trove of information concerning early Neolithic life. The subsequent Neolithic trackways that crossed the marsh and fenwood, and the platforms built on island shores, may seem run-of-the-mill beside the Sweet Track, but they and the number of stray finds from the third millennium bc enable us to observe people adapting to the changing wetland environment, following certain preferred routes from shoreline to shoreline, and developing a sophisticated use of the surrounding woodlands (chapters 4 and 5).

The earlier part of the second millennium bc shows a way of life essentially similar to that of the Neolithic. The relatively low number of structures from the period 2000–1400 bc is not necessarily due to a decline in exploitation of the marshes, for stray finds of flint and wood testify to human presence, and the environmental evidence for the dominance of raised bog indicates that built pathways may not have been necessary for access at this time. In the later second millennium, trackway building increased again in frequency, in response to changing surface conditions (chapter 6). The pollen record shows a steadily increasing impact of farmers on the dryland forest cover, perhaps a reflection of a growing population. Stray finds of bronze tools and weapons suggest that metal was coming into general use, some considerable time after the technical beginning of the Bronze Age, but its use does not appear to permit or promote any great change in the exploitation of wetland resources.

Moving forward through the first millennium bc, the record becomes increasingly patchy in one sense, in that much of it has been lost through early peat-cutting, at a time when archaeology was non-existent. In another respect, it becomes greatly augmented with the late first millennium settlements of Glastonbury and Meare (chapter 7). These sites contain structural evidence, a wide range of material culture, both organic and inorganic, and plant and animal remains indicative of economic and industrial processes. They rank with the Sweet Track as the outstanding discoveries from the Levels, thanks to the varied and detailed information that they add to the contemporary dryland record.

With Glastonbury and Meare we reach the end of the prehistoric record. It is not our aim to present the archaeology of Roman and later times, but it may be of interest to note that the fragmentary record, which is all that is left to us by early peat-cutters, shows little change in people's activities in the Levels over the next thousand years or more. The occupation at Meare probably continued for several centuries, and the wetlands were known to those who buried hoards of Roman coins in pewter vessels in the peat (see chapter 2). It seems, however, that the wetland environment exerted a stronger influence than any cultural change, however drastic the latter, and neither the Roman Conquest nor the invasions of the Dark Ages are reflected in the peat, although there may have been farming, with concomitant drainage, on the clay soils to west and north. People were present, but their actions remained conditioned by the wetland, and were to remain so for many centuries.

Medieval exploitation

In the light of this, a knowledge of early historic exploitation of the Levels may help to broaden our understanding of prehistoric life in the region. Settlements of the Levels recorded in the Domesday Book were spread along the slopes of the hills, and on the islands, but population was low in comparison with upland Somerset; tenancies in the Levels were only half those of the Polden Hills and the raised coastal belt. Plough-teams, representing arable farming, were rare, as were mills for grinding the corn. But the Levels had much meadowland and the highest density of cows in the county. Fishing was an important wetland activity, and Domesday records that the three fisheries at Meare occupied ten fishermen; their yield is unnoted, but two fisheries elsewhere in the Levels produced 6000 eels annually.

From the late twelfth to the early fourteenth century, the cartularies, rents and court rolls say much more about the Levels, and constantly refer to different types of land-holdings, from pools and seasonal pastures to flood-free arable lands; one example lists 40 acres of meadow, 77 acres of pasture, 8 acres of moor, and 16 acres of marsh. Patches of open water, whether natural watercourses or pools, provided fish, eel, fowl, reeds and rushes in varying and seasonal quantities. The fisheries were still important, especially those around plate 6
Meare Pool and near Burrow Bridge, and their annual payments to the abbey at Glastonbury included 7000 eels. Weirs were built on most of the watercourses, to hold back the ordinary waters, but these often flooded the moors and there are records of destruction of the weirs by irate commoners, as well as by the rival bishops and abbots of Wells and Glastonbury. Salmon and eel were common catches, but roach, perch, bream, pickerel, pike, flounder and tench were also taken. Water-fowl were important, as they had been in the Iron Age. Reference may be found, for example, to swans, geese and heron, and seasonal migrants were among the anticipated benefits of the waters and woods of the Levels. Rushes and reeds are less often recorded, although one of the duties of peasants was to gather reeds for the lord of the manor.

The watery nature of the Levels in the thirteenth century is clearly indicated by the duties of Robert Malerbe, 'water bailiff' of Glastonbury. Supervisor of the abbey vineyard at Panborough, he had to convey by boat the produce of this vineyard and of two others, at Meare and Pilton, to Glastonbury. He was also charged with the conveyance of the abbot and his men and his cook, his huntsmen and hounds, in fact everything that could be carried on the water, to abbey properties at Meare, Brent, Godney, Butleigh, Andersey and Stanton. Malerbe was required to go to Meare three times a week, and daily in Lent, for fish, and to act as coroner in the frequent cases of drowning. Although this record is illuminating for the medieval period, its contrast with that of the present day will also be obvious. Whether such an intricate network of water communication existed in any prehistoric period is uncertain, but the discovery of several dugout canoes makes it a possibility.

Water, though a source of livelihood, could also be a problem, and weirs and mill-races were not always effective. In 1490 a mill built by the Bishop of Wells was said to hinder navigation on the river Tone; the response was:

all the summer season the water is so lowe and so many shelpes and barges in the ryver between our myll and Taunton, that it is not possible to convey eny bote that way; and in the wynter season the meadows be so filled and replenysshed with water, that the bootes may go over at every place, so that they shall not be lett by the myll.

The medieval Levels had other resources to exploit, which gave less trouble to landowners than the uncontrollable waters. In the valley of the Brue, turbary rights were carefully regulated by the Abbot and the Bishop, and the collection of wood was also controlled. In 1337, the Dean of Wells took proceedings against Robert Gyan who had cut down many alder trees on Stan Moor; after Robert had been physically punished, he was granted six boatloads of brushwood each year, to be taken under supervision. Valuable stands of alder were guarded on Walton, Street and Aller Moors in the Brue valley, as well as on Sedgemoor.

There was a difference between taking brushwood and felling trees for building. The former was in effect a coppicing system, or harvest (see p. 86), but the latter meant destruction of the woodland. In 1241, the commoners of Godney Moor cut down eighty trees, and then 130 more, to repair bridges which they needed to maintain their rights to pasture, fuel and sedge on the moor; they were subsequently penalized for the act.

Hardly part of our concept of wild wetlands today, the greatest resource of all was not fish, or turf, or wood, but pasture, for, as at the time of the Domesday Book, parts of the Levels provided the richest grazing anywhere in Somerset. This was somewhat unreliable, as winter floods always inundated the moors, and spring and summer floods could occur, but most of the small settlements on the slopes and islands had intercommoning rights, and there were many complex disputes about territories, seasonal use, and over-stocking; in 1243, Geoffrey de Langelegl had to answer the Abbot as to why he had 'one hundred and fifty goats and twenty oxen and cattle beyond the number which he and his ancestors were wont always to have, to wit, sixteen oxen only.' The grazing rights held on the Brue valley moors were subject to the control of the Bishop of Wells and Abbot of Glastonbury, and conflicts were as regular as the floods. In the fourteenth century, the Bishop demolished some of the Glastonbury dykes and sluices in the northern Levels which had caused his crops to be flooded; the matter was not helped by deliberate firing of the moor all the way from Burtle Priory to Glastonbury, perhaps with the intention of burning the Abbey itself. The Abbot of course retaliated, and peace once more descended only when the northern Brue valley was divided into two parts in the fourteenth century; the line exists today as a parish boundary, and its rhyne is called Bounds Ditch. The incident underlines a great seasonal variation, from winter floods to summer dryness severe enough to allow firing of the moorland.

Land values in the medieval period are of some interest, because they show the importance of seasonal pasture and winter fodder supplies, in a land capable of yielding great wealth yet subject to the vagaries of the weather. For a farmer at this time, a poor supply of fodder and a lengthy period of inundation of his pasture, meant severe impoverishment and often starvation. By judicious ditching, rough pasture could be turned to meadow for hay, and the highest land values were attached to meadowland. At Glastonbury, pasture was 2d–6d an acre, arable 4d–10d an acre, and meadow 12d–13d an acre. At Meare, the meadows were still poor due to repeated flooding but elsewhere, as at Shapwick, 17 per cent of the manorial land was meadow, which contributed 55 per cent of the total income.

One aspect of local economies, which is as clear from the medieval records as it is from the archaeological evidence, is that they were mixed. No group relied solely on the exploitation of the wetland resources, and islands such as Edington Burtle or Meare-Westhay were put to good use. This point is well illustrated by the tithes due from Meare to the Abbot of Glastonbury's representative: 'tithes of calves, pigs, geese, flax, hemp, milk, cheese, wool, lambs, eggs, gardens, or curtilages, reed-walks, mills, pullets, and pigeons, from the tenants of the abbot and convent, parishioners there.'

There is much else of interest in the medieval records, and much still to be analysed. Recent work on Saxon charters, for example, has demonstrated the great potential of this source for landscape studies in the region. Our purpose in including the above paragraphs in a work essentially about the prehistoric wetlands has been to give a flavour of life in the region before drainage gave man the upper hand. From 4000 bc to the end of the Middle Ages, man perfected the art of living with and off the wetland. Subsequently, he began to control the waters, though even today not with complete certainty. Our work, described in the following chapters, has focused on the earlier part of the wetland period, when people adjusted to the ever-changing wetland conditions, and developed a rich life based on the diverse resources of the region. Just in case we have overstated the picture in emphasizing the natural wealth of the Levels, let us conclude this section with a reminder that, for some, there has always been another attitude: 'Agues, fevers, and other diseases arising from marsh miasmata, were the constant pest of the country, and rendered a residence in these low marshy situations, highly prejudicial to the health of its inhabitants.' (1836) The trackways that prehistoric people built, in great measure the subject of this book, were at least in part a response to such conditions, a way out of the Levels as well as a way in.

2 Bog-trotting: the development of archaeology in the Levels

> Yews, alders, birches, and willows, lying in all directions, at
> the depth of from one to five feet below the surface . . . but
> which being exposed to air soon crumble into pieces.

As we have seen in chapter 1, peat-cutting in the Levels was well-established by
the Middle Ages, and although the eighteenth-century comment quoted above
may refer to natural fenwood in the peat, the description would fit some of the
prehistoric structures we have excavated in the past ten years or so, especially
the various platforms of the Neolithic and Bronze Age. Without doubt, many
ancient finds were made by the commoners, the tenant-farmers, the
landowners, and latterly the professional peat-cutters, and only a few were
recorded, and fewer preserved. Nonetheless there is some record of old
discoveries, and for the Levels as for most other parts of Britain, these tend to
be associated with individual antiquaries.

fig. 2   In about 1834, the tenant of Honeygore Farm (which lies on a small sand-
bed between the islands of Westhay and Burtle) was cutting a rhyne when he
uncovered a line of split alder trees laid side by side deep in the peat. The
matter was disregarded until 1864 when a new owner of the estate heard of the
find, uncovered a length of the structure and invited the Somerset
Archaeological and Natural History Society to inspect the find. In 1873, a
further length was excavated and this marked its real discovery, as C. W.
Dymond, a Fellow of the Society of Antiquaries, was invited to view and to
publish the structure. His report appeared in 1880, and is simply called 'The
fig. 6   Abbot's Way'. The structure was a wooden trackway which was laid over a
raised bog to form a dry route between the large sand island of Burtle and the
rock island of Westhay, a distance of 3 km. Dymond was an acute and
enquiring observer, and in his report he wrote of the discovery of the structure
in 1834, its alignment and its character. He wondered if the track could have
been built by an Abbot of Glastonbury, to link the Burtle priory to the Meare
monastic estate. As the track was buried by 2 m of peat in places, Dymond was
unconvinced of its monastic attribution and name: 'If the title be ancient, it is
not a little singular that it should have survived the long inhumation – certainly
of several centuries; and if it be not, it is almost equally difficult to imagine how
it can have been given to an object known only to those who would not be apt
to hit upon the designation [i.e. the peat-cutters], who were ignorant of its

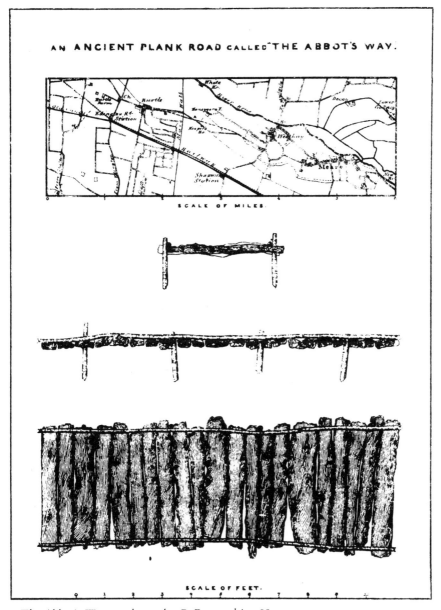

6 *The Abbot's Way, as drawn by C. Dymond in 1880.*

bearings, or who regarded the discovery as so unimportant that they did not reveal it for nearly a generation.' We do not know who assigned the name to this ancient track, and it is possible that it was first discovered not in 1834 but during the great drainage and diversion works carried out by the Glastonbury Abbey estates in the thirteenth century. If so, the name 'Abbot's Way' might have been given by the abbey workers, and perpetuated by irregular reminders of its existence through ditch cleaning across the moor. Dymond talked about 'the sea of speculation' concerning the name and lamented the absence of knowledge about peat growth, and the lack of care in recording positions and depths of the many finds of coins and other objects then being discovered in the turbaries. He was rather hard on the Rev. W. Stradling of Chilton Polden who had collected many artifacts, mislaying the provenance of most of them, and who concocted various schemes such as hurricanes to explain the old oak and yew trees found in the depths of the bog. Dymond's work on the Abbot's Way was well in advance of its time; he provided a clear description, plans and sections, map and measured positions of the structure, and his report was used by subsequent workers, namely Bulleid, Godwin and ourselves.

plate 7

Arthur Bulleid

The man who made the greatest contribution to the prehistory of the Levels was Arthur Bulleid. His major work was at the Glastonbury Lake Village, but there were many other discoveries, and it was his presence in the area that promoted interest in the ancient things that were uncovered by peat-cutters and farmers. As late as 1933 he reported on the Abbot's Way, and noted that he had seen it exposed in a roadside ditch in 1883, that is, fifty years earlier! At that time (1883) he was twenty years old, living in Glastonbury where his father, J. G. L. Bulleid, had already instilled in his son an interest in the antiquities of the region. Arthur Bulleid's 1933 paper is noted again below, as it provided impetus for our work and that of others in the Levels.

In 1888, while a medical student at Bristol, Bulleid read Ferdinand Keller's pioneer work on the discoveries of waterlogged settlements in the Swiss lakes, *The Lake Dwellings of Switzerland*. He came to the opinion that similar sites might well be preserved in the agreeably wet conditions of the Somerset peats, and so he set out to search the region. His own account of this search and its rewards cannot be improved upon:

For four years as opportunities occurred, the moorlands were explored looking for probable sites, more particularly in the peat-cutting localities of the Shapwick and Edington Burtle Turbaries. On a Wednesday afternoon in March, 1892, when driving across the moor from Glastonbury to Godney, a field was noticed to be covered with small mounds, an unusual feature in a neighbourhood where the conformation of the land is for miles at a dead level. On the following Sunday afternoon the field was visited, and anticipations were agreeably realized by picking up from the numerous mole-hills a number of pottery fragments, a whetstone, and pieces of bone and charcoal. The same evening in course of conversation a valued friend and neighbour, Mr Edward Bath, became interested in the matter, and having intimated that he believed the field belonged to him, a note arrived the following morning to confirm this, with permission to dig, subject to making arrangements with the tenant. This was done, and a week or two later tentative excavations took place by digging trenches into two of the mounds. The sections exposed clay floors with hearths, supported by massive timber substructures. Quantities of bone and antler, and a beautifully polished jet ring or bead, were among the relics discovered during these preliminary investigations. As the water-level was still high and flooded the trenches, it was deemed advisable to postpone the exploration until the summer. In the meantime the matter was brought before the Glastonbury Antiquarian Society, and a fund was started with the object of making a systematic examination of the site, and Mr Edward Bath generously made a gift of five acres of land (including the site of the village) to the Glastonbury Antiquarian Society. Investigations were begun towards the end of July, 1893, and were continued each year from May to October until 1898, when there was an unavoidable interruption in the work for five years. Excavations were resumed again in the summer of 1904, when Mr H. St. George Gray, F.S.A., happily joined the writer as joint director of the work until its termination in 1907.

plates 8, 9

Gray came to Glastonbury having trained with General Pitt-Rivers on his meticulous excavations in Dorset, and Bulleid and Gray formed a complementary team, Bulleid with his interests in geology as well as archaeology, Gray with his emphasis on detailed recording and artifacts. Both scientific input and stratigraphical concepts were quite new, and well in advance of contemporary work elsewhere.

During the work at Glastonbury (chapter 7), Bulleid received a parcel containing a potsherd, a spindle-whorl and a whetstone, from Stephen Laver, a farmer who lived near Westhay (incidentally, it was a Laver, of Honeygore Farm, who had first brought the Abbot's Way to C. W. Dymond's attention). Bulleid wrote back to Laver asking to be shown the site from where the finds had come, but his letter was lost. After a time (several weeks), Bulleid determined to find the site unaided:

Realizing that a farmer who rented land liable to flooding would place his hay stack on a mound or raised piece of ground, it was only necessary therefore when searching for the site to examine the hay stacks in the locality of Westhay and Meare. This was done systematically, and on the third Sunday's walk the site was discovered. Not only was the site found, but from the side of a ditch which happened to cut through the margin of one of the dwelling-mounds, fragments of a large pot were protruding.

plate 10

All of this was done while Bulleid was still a medical student, and he was sorely tempted to abandon his studies and become an archaeologist full-time. During his early work at Glastonbury, he met a young lady whose hand was promised by her father if Bulleid would persevere with his medical career. This he did, pursuing his practice near Bath, and his archaeology in the Levels. Harry Godwin wrote of Arthur Bulleid:

Doctor, archaeologist, geologist and artist he remained intensely cultivated, critical and human, utterly devoted to his wife but pretending that it was she who had kept him from an ideal life of archaeological research. I have always counted it as one of the major benefits and pleasures of the Somerset investigations that they brought me into contact with so distinguished and lovable a man.

The work and discoveries at Glastonbury were published in two sumptuous volumes within a very few years of the excavations, and they remain as important today as then. Looking ahead at our work which is described in chapters 3–7, although we today can claim to have developed an interdisciplinary project, Bulleid certainly foreshadowed us in his Glastonbury work. Indeed, he had three Fellows of the Royal Society to report on the plants, birds and mammals from the site, and he did not shy away from strong criticism of one of them (chapter 7). He was not so fortunate in his Meare work, and only the western part of the settlement was published, covering the work of Bulleid and Gray in the fifteen seasons they worked between 1910 and 1932. In 1933, Bulleid wrote his paper on discoveries in the peatfields, including the Abbot's Way, and it was in this year that he (aged seventy) and H. St. George Gray (aged sixty) began digging at the eastern Meare settlement; the work ended in 1956 with Arthur Bulleid only recently deceased, and with no prospect of publication by Gray who had acknowledged twenty-five years earlier that he was never likely to be able to publish all of his work even then. Nonetheless, both Bulleid and Gray had worked in the wetlands of Somerset for over fifty years, and both lived to be over ninety; perhaps it was the peat that enabled them to remain active for so long.

Bulleid's contribution to the prehistory of the Levels is not restricted to the 'lake villages', and in 1937 he and Wilfrid Jackson wrote a lengthy paper on the geological character of the Burtle beds of Somerset, establishing their Pleistocene age as well as indicating that the Shapwick Heath burtle had been later occupied by Mesolithic hunters and gatherers. This was a subject taken up by Stephen Dewar in his own pioneering work on the Levels (see below).

It is difficult for us to avoid reference once again to Bulleid's 1933 paper, because in this he described other structures buried in the peat, including the plate 11 Bronze Age Meare Heath track. He had seen this first in 1890 during his search for the lake villages, but it was then lost until peat-cutting began to destroy it along much of its length. Bulleid made numerous sorties into the peatfields to record the exposures, and published his sections and descriptions of the timbers. These formed the basis for our own work (chapter 6) and that of Harry Godwin.

Sir Harry Godwin

If Bulleid made the greatest contribution to archaeological discoveries in the Levels, then Sir Harry Godwin, Professor of Botany at Cambridge, is his equal in environmental studies of the bog, without which the structures would lack context and meaning. Bog is a word which is commonly applied to any area where the surface is so saturated with water that a passer-by will sink over his or her boot-tops, but in reality the word should mean wet peat, acid in character and forming a home for bog mosses, especially *Sphagnum*, and various flowering plants such as cotton-grass, sundew and bog asphodel, all of whose partially decayed remains form the peat on which further generations of the bog plants live. The word moss is sometimes applied to an area of bog because *Sphagnum* is so common there, but in the Levels the various areas of bog have been termed Heath, Moor, Waste or Level.

When Godwin first undertook his work on peats and pollen, the Levels were barely known as true peatland, and it was not until he saw an advertisement in the *Manchester Guardian* for the annual excavation at Meare that Godwin visited the Levels. Here he at once established good relations with Bulleid who recognized the value of detailed environmental analyses of the peats. While at Meare in 1936, Godwin heard of a find of Roman coins on Shapwick Heath, and went with Bulleid and the finder to the site. It was here that Godwin realized that Shapwick Heath was not a dry heath but a well-preserved raised bog, containing unique evidence for past vegetational changes and affording opportunities to develop the science of peat stratigraphy and pollen analysis.

From that moment, he made frequent expeditions to the Levels from his base in Cambridge, establishing a Cambridge connection that has existed for almost fifty years now. Godwin writes of his first introduction to the acid boglands: 'thus began a delightful involvement with what might light-heartedly be called bog-trotting, although heaven knows, there can be few natural communities less adapted to sustain trotting than those of the squelchy rain-fed mires!'

From the first, he and a host of research students (later to be spread across the world as professors and heads of Departments of Botany) carried out borings to the base of the peat, and examination of the thousands of sections (or heads) cut by peatsaw, knife and spade on Shapwick and Meare Heaths. These established and confirmed time and again the basic succession of deposits: at base, soft blue-grey clay of marine-estuarine origin, followed by *Phragmites* reed swamp, fenwood and *Sphagnum-Calluna-Eriophorum* raised bog, the last divisible into a lower, darker, more humified peat and an upper, paler, absorbent peat, the division sometimes associated with a major flooding horizon with *Cladium* giant sedge. These phases are fundamental to the prehistory of the Levels and are more fully discussed where relevant in this book.

Godwin's work with Bulleid at once led him into the archaeology of the area, and it is much to his credit as a scientist that he pursued the artifacts as rigorously as he approached his basic aim: the elucidation of the peat. His field-work in the peat-cuts was occasionally enlivened by adders (chapter 6) as well as by contact with numerous men working as hand-cutters or turners, and his investigations on the open pastureland, where he made many borings, were sometimes equally energetic: 'The field-work was often made exciting by the habit of keeping bulls along with the cows in the open pastures and one instantly had to estimate the defensive potential of a steel peat auger or one's ability (in gum-boots) to jump a 10-foot [3 m] rhyne.' We have found a 2-m ranging rod equally useful in fending off inquisitive or offended bulls, and comment on rhyne-jumping appears later.

Godwin's involvement in the peatfields of the Levels coincided with an

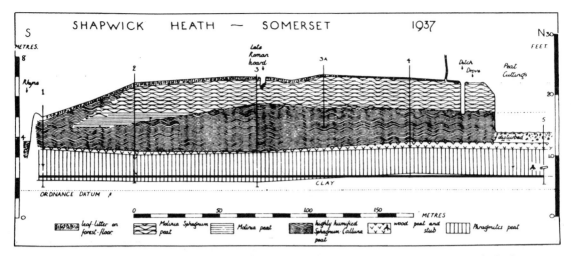

7 H. Godwin's peat section from Shapwick Heath, as observed in 1937, with the basic sequence of clay, reed swamp, fenwood, and raised bog. The horizontal line marks the approximate level of the peat in 1985, lowered through peat-cutting.

expansion of cutting in old areas, and the opening of new fields in land previously wooded or used as pasture. He was therefore able to see sequences of deposits which were more or less complete, with all the vegetational phases represented. Since then, of course, much has disappeared, and a look at fig. 7 will show the difference between the peat section seen by Godwin in 1937 on Shapwick Heath and that observable today; almost 5 m of peat have been cut away, with raised bog deposits the first to go, then fenwood, and finally most, or all, of the reed swamp peats.

One of the areas examined by Godwin in the 1940s was the Westhay Level, where he was shown a series of brushwood tracks which he called Honeygore (after the farm) and Honeycat (a combination of Catcott Burtle and Honeygore farm). Our team subsequently worked in this complex, and found *fig. 18* Honeybee (which had beehives nearby), Honeydew (nearby sundew) and Honeypot (to maintain the tradition). The naming of sites in the Levels is complicated and neither Godwin nor we ever had any set of rules for the game. There is no system: often a farm will provide a suitable name (Blakeway track), or a finder (Foster's track), or a landowner (Baker Platform), or a peat company (Eclipse track).

Both Bulleid and Godwin were energetic and enthusiastic about their work. Bulleid searched for four years before finding his lake village, and Godwin too showed his mettle in seeking for new exposures of peat or structures. In 1944, he was told of a previously unknown trackway which ran 'straight as a die' north–south at Blakeway farm north of Westhay. He records: 'Since no surface trace remained, and we had only a general idea of location, Roy Clapham and I, in determined mood, sunk a row of thirty-six borings at 1-ft [0.3 m] intervals across the presumed line of the track and eventually we made six borings, only a few inches apart, each containing at the same depth the typical clear yellow uniform wood of hazel.' This was then excavated, dated to the third millennium bc, and published as the Blakeway track, a structure of young hazel rods which gave the earliest evidence in the world for a coppiced woodland, a fact unnoted by any one (including ourselves) for over a decade (chapter 5).

In 1942, Godwin and Clapham had been as determined to find the Abbot's Way, and various lines of borings were made along the route as noted by Dymond and Bulleid. In this case, however, the search was not successful and it was only in 1961 that the structure was found; its history from this date more fairly falls into a later section of this chapter.

In 1936, Godwin had been informed of the discovery on Shapwick Heath of a late Roman hoard of 120 silver coins dating to AD 410, together with a pewter   plate 13
saucer and platter. The next year, another hoard was found 2 m away with 125 silver coins in a pewter jug of AD 388. In the next year, only 3 m away, was found a third hoard of 1170 bronze coins in a pewter bottle, dating AD 320–390. A fourth hoard, buried 10 m away, consisted of pewter and bronze bowls with a bronze-covered wooden tankard, dating AD 400. Since this period of peat-cutting, three further Roman hoards have been found some distance away, one in peat-cutting, one by a metal detector and the third by a rotovating machine which sprayed out hundreds of coins in all directions. It is evident that all the hoards were buried in the raised bog surface by the owners, who dug narrow holes, placing the objects into the wet peat, and covering them with heaps of peat and bog vegetation. These discoveries suggested to Godwin that peat formation had ceased sometime in the mid-first millennium AD, although we do not know how much of the final raised bog peats were lost to early peat-cutters.

Radiocarbon dating was another technique in which Godwin was very active. With the development of the Cambridge laboratory (later and most appropriately named the Godwin Laboratory), samples of peat and wood from the Levels could be dated and shown to form a logical sequence, from c. 3500 bc to c. ad 400, in which the many structures and finds could be fitted. But Godwin was more concerned with peat stratigraphy, and one of the finds made by early peat-cutters had puzzled him. This was a logboat of oak found   plate 12
in the widening and deepening of a ditch at the Shapwick railway station, and Godwin wondered what a substantial dugout canoe was doing on top of the raised bog. Bog pools were no real answer, and it was not until years later that the recognition of flooding horizons in the peats showed that, at the time, extensive floodwaters had ranged across this part of the Levels (chapters 6 and 7), and that the presence of a boat was entirely logical; the latter had been abandoned on the edge of a small 'island' of fenwood growing on the peat, in the closing centuries bc. In 1963, we excavated around the 'island' edge, to find nothing but natural interlaced fenwood roots and drowned stems and branches.

Near the island, Godwin had found a scatter of elk droppings buried in first millennium bc peat, thus showing a very late survival of the animal in southern England, and providing one of the few animal 'tracks' in bone-dissolving acid peats. The question of animal identification is pursued at various points in this book, and the 'tracks' are indeed varied (see chapters 3, 4 and 6).

In 1944, Godwin met Stephen Dewar, a man of great enthusiasm and dedication, and they at once began collaborative work on Shapwick Heath. Dewar was a retired tea-planter living on the Poldens, and he established a very close contact with the peat-cutters, receiving information about their discoveries and often donating bottles of refreshment in exchange. He made numerous finds himself, among them several Bronze Age trackways, but his greatest contribution was in his proximity to the cuttings and the regularity of his visits. He helped maintain the interest in the relics from the peat (following Bulleid's example) and of about thirty tracks or small finds recorded in 1963, over twenty had been investigated in the field by either Godwin or Dewar, or both.

fig. 8 Bulleid's work on the geology of the Burtle sand-beds has been briefly noted and he recorded in 1937 that H. S. L. Dewar had collected Mesolithic flints from the Shapwick Burtle, a small sand-bed lying near the Polden Hills. Dewar

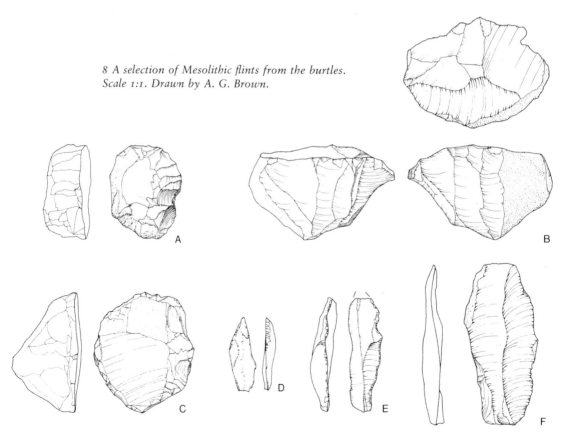

8 A selection of Mesolithic flints from the burtles.
Scale 1:1. Drawn by A. G. Brown.

was obviously active in the Levels before meeting Godwin, although it was their collaborative work that was so rewarding for archaeology. The flints from this burtle-bed are only one of perhaps ten such assemblages now known through our own work, and they represent the earliest human traces in the Levels proper. At the time of their making (probably in the fifth millennium bc) the Levels were intertidal mud-flats, with swamplands here and there, and dense forests on the rock islands and hillslopes. Doubtless the resources of the Levels were then extensive, ranging from fish and fowl in the waters to deer and pig in the woodlands. No settlement sites with structural information have been identified, and probably most were overtaken by the flooding-in of the blue-grey marine clays which ride up the sides of the islands and totally overwhelmed a number of them. Such sites remain for future investigation, and Christopher Norman has already begun working on the flint scatters on Sedgemoor.

Origins of the Somerset Levels Project

In 1962, one of us (J. M. C.), newly arrived in Cambridge as an assistant lecturer, was introduced to the Levels by Professors Harry Godwin and Grahame Clark. Clark was just completing his studies on the Neolithic bows from the peat (chapter 4), and Godwin his collaborative work with Stephen Dewar. Both studies were published in the *Proceedings of the Prehistoric Society* for 1963. We met Dewar on Shapwick Heath, scene of many of his discoveries, saw him in an 'exchange' with a peat-cutter, and visited the burtle-bed where he at once found a few Mesolithic flints. In the same year, J. M. C. began work on the Heath, excavating the remnants of a late Bronze Age track (the Viper's, as named by Godwin) and discovering and excavating another track (the Platform) virtually single-handed (chapter 7). Samples of the wood and peat were brought to Cambridge for identification by Godwin and his assistants in the Botany School, and this was the beginning of a long and fruitful collaboration with that School and its Sub-Department of Quaternary Studies, at first with Godwin and then with Professor Richard West as its directors.

In 1964, a series of meetings with Dewar was held and we plotted our campaign on both Shapwick Heath (for surveys and tracing of Bronze Age tracks) and on the Westhay Level, where Dymond, Bulleid and Godwin had all worked on the Abbot's Way. Very active peat-cutting was being undertaken by the E. J. Godwin Peat Company (no relation), and both Mr Godwin and his son-in-law Ricky Rowland at once offered assistance, and the latter showed me the exposures of Neolithic tracks recently seen by Harry Godwin. The identical surname of E. J. and Harry was a regular source of comment and Harry Godwin records that E. J. displayed 'a cordiality that covered roast duck for "impromptu" lunch and highly effective refreshment against the rigours of the open peat face.'

plate 7

The Abbot's Way ran through one section of a peatfield, and was excavated with a small team of Cambridge undergraduates. The site was within 100 m of the spot where the Abbot's Way had first been seen approximately 130 years previously. As we moved across the peatfields to the east, observing the track in numerous sections, we made several other small examinations. Some of the split alder transverses were lifted and carted back to Cambridge for conservation in the University Museum of Archaeology and Ethnology. All of this work, in fact the first ten years of work in the Levels, was aided by the Crowther-Beynon Fund of the University of Cambridge, and its support still continues.

plate 14

In the winter of 1964 and through 1965 and 1966, we managed to trace the Abbot's Way across the pasture fields between the peat works and the island of Westhay, a distance of about 1000 m. As the track lay under the grassland, we drilled for it (in as determined a way as Harry Godwin had done years before) and occasionally excavated to make sure we were bumping onto the track wood with our post-holer, and not any old tree root. Some larger excavations were also undertaken, again with Cambridge students, including Joan Taylor (now Reader in Archaeology at Liverpool), and she continued to work in the Levels for four or five years. As the work progressed, it became obvious that some more established form of environmental help was needed, and we approached Alan Hibbert (later to become Professor at Portsmouth) who was newly arrived in the Cambridge Sub-Department of Quaternary Studies. He at

---

Colour plates (*pages 35, 36*)

V Excavations on the Sweet Track, immediately prior to site photography, with all planks and boxes removed. Only toe-boards are used for final cleaning.

VI A machine at work on Tinney's Ground, cutting, lifting and stacking the mumps of peat which are then left to dry. In the foreground can be seen the remnants of a Bronze Age brushwood track, one of a multitude found in this field (see chapter 6).

VII The God-Dolly, a figure carved from ashwood, found beneath the Bell track.

VIII Axe of jadeite from the Sweet Track, *c.*3200 bc.

IX The Abbot's Way. Reconstruction of the road of *c.*2000 bc on the Ancient Monument. The site is open to the public.

V

VI

VII

VIII

IX

once agreed to collaborate in the Levels, and brought his considerable skill and enthusiasm to the studies of wood and especially pollen for a period of ten years, during which time the work continued to develop into new and more intensive lines of enquiry.

Harry Godwin had spoken of his ability to jump a 3-m rhyne (in gumboots) to escape a bull, and we witnessed just such an Olympian feat during one of our early digs on the Abbot's Way. Separated from the modern road by a wide rhyne, we were spotted one day by a traveller who stopped his car and made his way over the fields towards our site, clearly intending to visit. We watched as he, in dark grey business suit, neared the rhyne which we knew was wide and deep. He paused, considered the matter and turned away. Before we could shout encouragement, directions, or warning, he swivelled, ran to the rhyne, leaped, and fell straight in; amazed and convulsed, we could do nothing as he clambered out on the same side and made his squelchy way back to his car and his business appointment.

By 1966, the upper peats on Shapwick Heath, where Dewar and Godwin had worked, had been totally removed by peat-cutting, and although we occasionally searched the heads, there was no sign of any ancient structure: little did we know what awaited us there. So instead we pursued the Neolithic tracks on the Westhay Level, first the Abbot's Way, which led us eventually, through the good fortune of meeting Maurice Bell and his sons on Westhay, to the Bell tracks, the God-Dolly, the Baker Platform and ancient beaver; the story of these discoveries is best reserved for chapter 4. Here we had the assistance of David Coombs (now Senior Lecturer at Manchester) and the long-continued collaboration with Andrew Fleming (now Reader at Sheffield) who bore the trials and tribulations of digging the Baker Platform with admirable fortitude. This was a complicated site full of wood, and access to the work was very difficult. Our rule, enforced by Andrew, was 'no feet on peat', which meant that all work was to be done from planks supported over the site by a system of boxes and interwoven planks (chapter 3). On one occasion, this rule was observed by an undergraduate who stood not on the peat but on the Neolithic wood. The spoil heap by now weighed several tons and it took him a long time to move it.

In 1968, our first paper was published, on the Abbot's Way and the Bell tracks, and from then on we tried to maintain a regular flow of papers on the collaborative work. In this year we met a successor to Stephen Dewar in the person of Colin Clements, who came to work at the Baker site, was struck by the attractions of the peat, and continued to work in the Levels for several years. In 1968, we suggested to Clements that he might follow up notes provided by Dymond in 1880, and Bulleid in 1933, which indicated that tracks existed far to the west, on Chilton Moor. This moor lies south of the largest sand island in the Brue valley: that of Burtle itself. Clements dug narrow slit trenches across several fields, and cleaned various ditch faces, and discovered a brushwood structure in the bank of the old Glastonbury Canal.

In the same year, the canal was widened and deepened by the river authority, and Clements and the machine operators kept a close watch as new

fig. 18 ditches were cut and the canal bank scraped. A series of structures was soon discovered, and further work revealed even more, so that the moor south of Burtle could be seen to contain short lengths of dozens of brushwood tracks and occasional platform-like structures. We carried out excavations on four of these, which were later dated to the third millennium bc.

Following this work, Clements turned to another track, the M5 motorway, although he later came back to the Levels, this time to Sedgemoor south of the Polden Hills. Here he worked with Christopher Norman who had made various discoveries of prehistoric wooden structures in drainage ditches around the sand islands of Chedzoy.

During the early spring of 1970, J. M. C. received a parcel in Cambridge from the Eclipse Peat Works, the company which had operated on Shapwick and Meare Heaths for decades, and which had years before retrieved and helped preserve the Neolithic longbows for Godwin and Grahame Clark. The parcel contained a piece of ash plank, clearly split from a large tree; with it was a note that it had been found in a deep ditch on Shapwick Heath. I hastened to the Levels to meet the finder, Raymond Sweet, and a small exploration soon revealed more of the same wood together with pegs still driven into the lower peats, and axed debris. A fine leaf-shaped arrowhead had already been found by Sweet nearby, as well as a hoard of flint flakes only 100 m away, lying about 1 m above the blue-grey clay at the base of the peat. It all looked Neolithic. In the summer of 1970, teams of students arrived and in addition to other sites we excavated a small part of the new structure, soon to be called the Sweet Track (chapter 3).

This was the first year in which we received support from the Maltwood Fund of the Royal Society of Arts. Mrs Maltwood had been a firm believer in the archaeological potential of the Somerset Levels, particularly as it related to the Glastonbury Tor and its more magical attributes, and her bequest of funds has been widely disseminated by a wise committee of the Royal Society of Arts. We have received generous support from the Society ever since this year of 1970.

Work on the Sweet Track in summer 1970 was very small-scale, but among the diggers was Bryony Orme, then a research student in London. In subsequent years, as supervisor and then co-director, she assumed a major role in all of the Levels work. By 1973, we had the beginnings of a multi-disciplinary team, with Alan Hibbert for pollen and peat, Ruth Jones (later Ruth Morgan) for tree-ring studies, and conservation still based in Cambridge, and we were asked by the Department of the Environment if we needed any financial help for our major excavations on the Sweet Track. We naturally agreed and with a modest grant of £1000 we undertook an enormous excavation at the Railway Site (see chapter 3 for the full account). On one momentous day, late in the dig, we were visited by Dr Geoffrey Wainwright, then the area inspector, who watched as our team worked steadily through torrential rain, and since that time our national support has been unswerving.

In 1973, the Somerset Levels Project was created, and it now combines the direct and continuing support of the Universities of Cambridge and Exeter, the Maltwood Fund of the Royal Society of Arts, the Department of the Environment (as was) and the Historic Buildings and Monuments Commission (as is). Many other bodies also help from time to time, including the Science and Engineering Research Council, the Natural Environment Research Council, the Society of Antiquaries of London and the Leverhulme Trust, but perhaps the greatest support comes from the major and minor peat companies who lend premises, land, machinery and manpower for our work.

As soon as the Project was created, we could afford to put student field archaeologists to work searching the peat-cuts, and we were at once rewarded with a multitude of discoveries all over the Brue valley. This work forms the basis of the chapters which now follow.

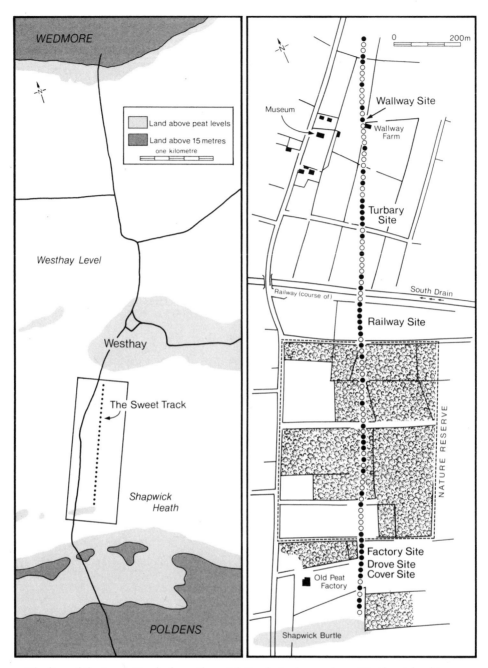

9 *The line of the Sweet Track, from Shapwick Burtle in the south, to Westhay island in the north. Solid circles indicate excavated sites; the major ones discussed in the text are named.*

3 A day's work: the Sweet Track

If you will tell me why the fen
appears impassable, I then
will tell you why I think that I
can get across it if I try.
(Marianne Moore 1956)

The wet winter months when peat-cutting ceases are the season of ditch-clearing in many parts of the Levels. Early in 1970, such work was going on around the edge of one of the large peatfields on Shapwick Heath, behind an old peat factory, when Ray Sweet discovered the first plank of the Early Neolithic Sweet Track. The story of our immediate visit has already been told in chapter 2, and this marked the beginning of almost fifteen years of work on this unusual and rewarding structure.

The track lay deep in the peats on Shapwick Heath, well below the levels at which Stephen Dewar had found the Bronze Age tracks, and as much as 4 m below the bog surface seen by Harry Godwin thirty years before. The loss of peat was due to cutting as well as to shrinkage of the bog. The track was clearly associated with Godwin's lowest peat-type, the *Phragmites* reed swamp, although there were also occasional stumps of birch and patches of moss and cotton-grass.

The marsh was rich in wild life and varied plants. A sea of reeds dominated the vegetation in summer, almost masking the few birch, willow and alder, and hiding from sight the sporadic pools of open water where currents flowed more strongly. There were no main rivers, rather a network of small streams and pools through which the water trickled westwards in summer, allowing pond weed and water-lilies to grow and water insects to flourish. In winter, and at other times of heavy rain, the network became a sheet of brown floodwaters sweeping down the reeds and uprooting the weaker trees. In these conditions, it would have been possible to see across the marsh from the foot of the Polden Hills to Westhay island, but in the summer the view was obscured by the tall, dense stands of *Cladium* and *Phragmites*. Most of the dryland was covered by deciduous forest at this period, and any clearings and paths were small and scattered, affording less of an open network in the sea of trees than the streams and pools provided among the reeds.

Radiocarbon Calibration	
0 bc	0 BC
	500
500	
	1000
1000	
	1500
1500	
	2000
2000	2500
	3000
2500	
	3500
3000	
4000	
	CALIBRATED
3500	
UNCALIBRATED	

41

In the summer of 1970, we excavated a short stretch of the track, not really knowing how it had been constructed; it was totally unlike anything we had seen in the Levels, or read about elsewhere. A perfect flint axe blade was found on the second day, lying beside the wood which was itself generally well-preserved, with gleaming golden bark intact and, at the end of each stem, the facets, cut to a sharp point, showing as clearly as the day they were made. We did not then know the age of the trackway, other than knowing it to be Neolithic, but as we uncovered it we had a very strong sense that we were the first people to see these timbers for several millennia.

Unlike other trackways, everything seemed novel and unusual, and we began to plan our campaign to trace the track across the peatlands, to assess its condition and to establish the likely threats to its survival. 'Sweet' was to prove a most appropriate name for a trackway that has captured the interest of many as 'the oldest road' and which has proved a constant stimulus to the development of our work. The demands of excavation, conservation, preservation, post-excavation and environmental work have been many, calling on all our resources and ingenuity, and resulting in new techniques in many fields. These aspects will be discussed in the following pages, after a brief survey of the sequence of work on the Sweet Track, work which has by no means ceased as the trackway continues to tax the brains of many.

Our aims were always to try to understand how the Sweet Track worked and why it was built, and to save as much of it as possible from peat-cutting and desiccation. We believed the track to run from near the Poldens in the south to the island of Westhay in the north, a distance of about 2 km, and we therefore searched along its presumed route, inspecting old ditches in the hope of seeing it in section. It was only when a new drainage ditch was cut in the summer of 1971, 600 m to the north of our first site, and near the old railway line, that we saw the track again. We were just in time. Our efforts to pin the spot down by measurements to adjacent large trees were foiled within days by the total felling of the whole woodland prior to a programme of massive peat-cutting. However, we asked the peat company to delay their cutting, and, of course, the Eclipse Peat Works did so, giving us every assistance. In 1972, we carried out a small excavation here, which yielded some particularly finely worked timbers and pegs, as well as many potsherds, including the remains of a complete pot with its wooden stirrer, abandoned beside the track where it had fallen. Later in 1972, we returned to the southern exposure, and since by now we had decided to name the sites after various landmarks, this became the Factory Site (as it lay behind an old peat-processing factory); the site to the north was near the Glastonbury to Highbridge railway line, recently axed, so it was known as the Railway Site. It sounded very industrial, but nothing could be less so than Shapwick Heath. We investigated the southern end of the track, as it entered the reed swamps off the Burtle Site, and later we also looked at the Copse Site and the Drove Site nearby, in advance of peat-cutting and serious drying of the whole western end of Shapwick Heath.

Our largest excavation was that of the Railway Site where we received our first indication that the Sweet Track was even more complex than suspected, with not one but two tracks built near or on top of one another. Many fine Neolithic artifacts were found here, of which more will be said below. Later on we moved farther northwards, to an emergency South Drain Site about to be destroyed in widening the Drain, then to the Turbary Site, and the Wallway Site, situated far to the north beside an abandoned farm. All the sites were given names running alphabetically from south (Burtle) to north (Wallway) as a glance at fig. 9 will show; this was initially fortuitous and subsequently deliberate.

As threats to the trackway increased, we decided that we should trace it along the full length and check on the condition of the wood from south to north. The tracing was carried out in 1980–81, principally filling in the line between the Factory and Railway Sites, as well as running north to the Westhay shore. The track was found to run in a remarkably straight line. Its condition varied considerably, some sections being well-protected by deep wet peats whereas others were at risk because of nearby drainage ditches or old peat-cutting which had reached to within centimetres of the track wood. Part of the track lay buried in the peats of the Shapwick Heath Nature Reserve, and our investigations were preliminary to a major attempt to preserve the structure here; this is described in chapter 8.

Excavation

Twelve years of excavation along the Sweet Track have evolved a pattern of work that copes with the many pressing demands of a waterlogged site. The decision to excavate has always been prompted by a threat to the structure: by peat extraction or the more insidious action of general drainage. We have been fortunate that all the landowners and tenants along the track line have readily given permission to excavate, and have held up their own work until ours was done. Co-operation on our part has meant at times digging in December or March, but that has had its compensations because the exposed wood then dries out less rapidly than in July sunshine. Once work starts on a site, it must be pushed through to completion as rapidly as possible, and we have found that 60 m is the maximum length that can be examined at any one time; the ideal length of site is 20–30 m: long enough to understand the structure yet short enough to keep a close watch on the excavation. Excavation teams have varied in their size and composition over the years from two (the authors) to about thirty. Volunteers have been mostly students, though not necessarily of archaeology, and a number have come from abroad. We have also been joined by professionals from other countries wishing to learn about the excavation and conservation of waterlogged wood. The Project's environmentalists have always been present, taking a share in the archaeological work as well as borrowing volunteers to assist in their sampling programmes.

The amount of overburden varies from site to site, according to the extent of previous peat-cutting. When deep, it has been removed by machine, courtesy of the peat company, and then by spading, courtesy of the volunteers. Once the higher parts of the structure have been located, spades are discarded for perspex spatulae, and the rule 'no feet on peat' is applied. On any waterlogged site, it is essential that people do not trample the surface; in the peat the weight of a person, even if placed carefully in an apparently vacant spot, will inevitably crush any wood hidden below. Therefore, everyone works from

plate V

toe-boards, which are pieces of wood the size of a bread-board, one for knees and one for toes, which spread their weight. As work proceeds and more wood is exposed, it is often easier, and safer, to work from planks set on wooden

plate 15

boxes to bridge the prehistoric structure. The digger is thus suspended directly

plate 17

over his or her work, delicately removing peat from wood using a spatula or bare fingers. Trowels are not used in the soft peats as sharp metal edges are unfeeling, and damage the wood. The perspex does little damage, and is relatively sensitive to changes in peat density. Bare fingers are best of all, sensing the wood before it is exposed and peeling away the peat covering to reveal an oak plank surface or the bark of an oblique peg without actually touching the structure at all. Each piece of wood is numbered, using metal or plastic labels attached by pins.

Once exposed, the wood has to be watered regularly, except during rainfall. After a week to ten days digging, when much wood is exposed, half the team may be engaged in keeping the track wet. Watering cans are used, and sponges to dribble water over a delicate piece, or soft hand-brushes, dipped in a bucket and shaken along a plank. Exposed wood which is not currently being cleaned is watered and then covered in polythene, and the whole site is covered at the

plate 18

end of the working day. Without polythene, we estimate that only a metre of track at a time could be exposed, recorded and lifted before the wood suffered from drying-out.

plate 19

The exposed structure is recorded by photography and by planning. The photography is always an anxious but exhilarating moment, as all the protective polythene is removed and puddles of water are mopped up, and the whole track is seen for perhaps the one and only time. The photograph must be taken rapidly, whatever the light conditions, and the polythene replaced on newly watered trackway as soon as possible. Planning is done at a scale of 1:10.

fig. 10

Relative heights are recorded by levelling such things as plank surfaces, peg tops, post tops, and artifacts; the angles of the pieces of wood may also be relevant for understanding the construction of the trackway and its state when engulfed by peat. These angles are recorded using an angle-indicator, a small device officially known as a declinometer, which enables us for example to note accurately whether a peg was at an angle of 30° or 45° or 80° to the horizontal.

Further essential recording takes place as the trackway is dismantled. By this time, the directors and specialists have made preliminary decisions regarding the fate of each piece of wood, and these are signalled to the lifting teams by a series of coloured pins stuck in the wood; a red pin, for example, means that a tree-ring sample is to be taken from a specific spot. Each lifting team consists of three or four people working together, with one person physically lifting the wood piece by piece out of the site, a second filling in a printed report card, a third dealing with samples and the fourth coping with emergency requests and digging over behind the lifter. The record cards ensure that certain information is noted, such as the dimensions of the piece, its associations and its surface character as well as the samples taken. Comments are written on woodworking details and any unusual features such as fungus zone lines, or a notch in a plank. About 5 cm length of wood is taken for species identification and for tree-ring analysis. Pieces with signs of beetle or fungal attack are sampled for the relevant specialists, and wood which exhibits an interesting growth characteristic (e.g. a coppiced heel) is put aside for further examination. Wherever possible, pieces in good condition are saved for conservation, with no on-site sampling, and the worked ends of pegs and posts are taken to the conservation laboratory.

The excavation ends with an empty site and a laboratory full of wood, stored in cold water tanks until it has been photographed. All pieces in a good enough state of preservation are then conserved (chapter 5). Meanwhile, sacks and boxfulls of samples are despatched to Exeter, Cardiff, London, Sheffield, Cambridge, or wherever else the specialist might be based, and then post-excavation work begins. Substantial peat samples are also taken, from around   plate 16 the trackway wood or in monoliths through and beside the structure, and used for analysis of pollen, macro-plant remains and beetles. Over the years, as we have developed the potential of the Sweet Track as a source of archaeological and palaeoenvironmental information, post-excavation studies have multiplied and become more sophisticated, but thanks to the commitment of those working on the different aspects, and to good funding, publication has not been delayed. And publication has been crucial, for the Levels structures epitomize the dictum that a site is undiscovered until it is published (see also chapter 7, re Meare); waterlogged wood cannot in any way be left exposed *in situ* for the public to see, or for archaeologists to study.

The Sweet Track revealed by excavation was an ingenious structure. The   plates 19, 20 aim of the Neolithic builders of the late fourth millennium bc was to provide a raised path across a wet reed swamp. They did this by putting a long pole or rail on the marsh surface, usually a slim straight trunk of ash, alder, hazel or elm. Pairs or groups of oblique pegs were then pushed or driven down into the soft unstable surface to either side of the rail, so that they crossed over it. The groups were set every metre or so, and upon the V formations thus created, the planks were placed. Balanced carefully, they made an effective walkway. The planks were supported about 40 cm above the rails, abutting end to end across 1800 m of marsh. Further stability was achieved by cutting notches in the underside edge of the planks, to lodge them firmly on a peg, and by the

TURBARY SITE

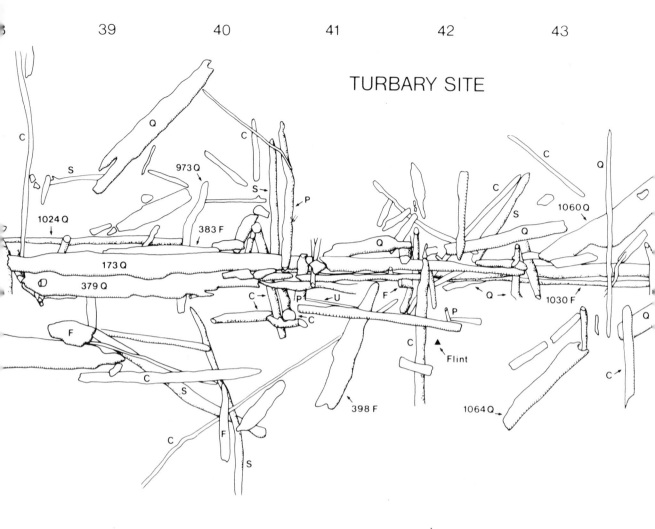

occasional vertical peg driven through a hole cut towards the end of a plank or driven down beside the plank.

    The Sweet Track had been preceded by the construction gang's own access track, roughly built to ease the bringing-in of material. This preliminary track, *plate 21* called the Post Track (rather illogically in terms of chronology), underlay the Sweet Track wherever the two paths crossed, and consisted in the main of marker posts driven in vertically every 3 m or so along the line, and heavy planks of ash and lime connecting the posts. The planks were rarely pegged, and do not seem to have been raised off the marsh surface. As the Post Track *plate 24* appeared to have been dismantled, and occasional characteristically heavy planks of lime and ash were found as rails in the Sweet Track, we considered that it had been plundered to build the later, straighter walkway. Since building our experimental Sweet Track reconstruction (chapter 5), we are quite sure that the Post Track was never more than a preliminary marking-out

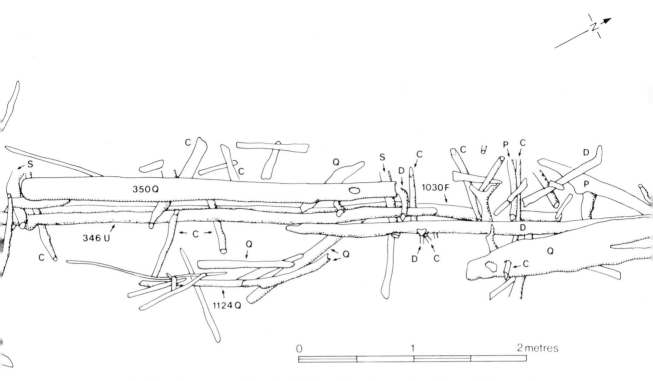

10 A Sweet Track plan. This section is from the Turbary Site, 38–50 m along the track. The trackway components are identified to species as follows: Q, 'Quercus' (oak); C, 'Corylus' (hazel); F, 'Fraxinus' (ash); U, 'Ulmus' (elm); P, 'Populus' (poplar); S, 'Salix' (willow); D, 'Cornus' (dogwood). Every piece of wood is numbered, but the plan here gives only those significant tree-ring sampled pieces, as well as a few other important elements. 379 at 39 m was a tangential oak plank with sapwood, and 383 also at 39 m was an ash plank felled after the trackway was built, and probably used to shore up a disintegrated stretch.

line and base from which to build the raised walkway, an interpretation supported by tree-ring analysis of samples taken from both tracks.

Environmental studies

Our understanding of the track structure has grown with each excavation, and with the experimental reconstruction. It has also been advanced by the varied environmental studies which have been made of the track wood and associated material. As far as possible, the different studies have been related to each other. For the beetle and plant macro-studies carried out for the Turbary Site, immediately adjacent samples were taken at intervals along the length of the site, with Maureen Girling taking one to extract and identify the insect remains, and Astrid Caseldine taking the other to examine the plant macrofossils. The results they obtained from samples taken where the track dipped slightly are of interest. The plants identified included several species of sedge, rush and reed, as expected, and rather more open-water plants than usual: the white water-lily, for example. Amongst the insects were diving beetles and whirligig beetles, and the giant spider *Dolomedes*, which had not been encountered before in any Levels samples. *Dolomedes*, the Raft Spider, has a body length of 25 mm and lives by and on permanent water, a fearsome creature hunting aquatic insects and small fish. Both plant and animal species therefore indicated a particularly wet spot in the marsh, and it was here that the trackway had been built with three superimposed rails instead of the usual one, presumably to cope with the increased wetness.

plate 22

plate 23

Insect remains survive well in the peat, but vertebrate skeletons usually decay rapidly and there is no direct evidence for the birds, amphibians and mammals of the Levels at the time the Sweet Track was built. Caseldine has found indirect evidence, however, for the presence of two small mammals. Her work on the plants included examination of the many hazelnuts discovered amongst the trackway timbers. These nuts are sometimes whole, sometimes broken, and were flooded in from the dryland edges (no hazel would grow in the reed fen) or dropped by travellers enjoying a quick snack. Two nuts from the Turbary Site had neat holes, with tooth-marks around the edge. Enquiries and comparison with modern samples established that one had been eaten by a dormouse and the other by a bank vole. We assume these particular nuts were flooded in from drier areas of the Levels, rather than discarded by hungry rodents as they travelled along the track.

The beetle identifications from the Sweet Track are used in the first instance to reconstruct local environmental conditions, as we saw above. But they can provide other sorts of information. Five of the species identified by Girling are no longer found in Britain, and four of these may have become extinct because of changes in climate. By examining the modern distribution of these four, *Oodes gracilis*, *Chlaenius sulcicollis*, *Anthicus gracilis* and *Airaphilus elongatus*, Girling has established their preference for more continental conditions, with colder winters and warmer summers than are normal in Somerset today. It is possible, therefore, that when the Sweet Track was built winter temperatures were 2–4° colder and summers 2–3° hotter than now.

The pollen grains preserved in the peat were blown in from the surrounding dryland as well as from the marshes. Pollen analyses can therefore be used to reconstruct both regional and local vegetation, and the several studies now made at different points along the line of the trackway give an indication that the dryland vegetation of the Shapwick burtle (south end) was not entirely similar to that of the Westhay island (north end). Hibbert and Beckett's analyses were made at the burtle end, and Caseldine's more recent ones near the centre and well to the north. Although all the analyses show that forest cover was partially cleared when the trackway was built, the southern pollen indicates a decline in elm and lime occurring perhaps a little earlier than to the north, and the overall pollen evidence for farming is stronger from the south than from the north. Hibbert also noted that it was relatively strong from the large sandy island of Edington Burtle, during this same episode of forest clearance. This could be because the Neolithic farmers cultivated the sandy burtle soils more intensively than the soils developed on the lias island; they certainly seem to have used the Shapwick burtle in such a way that elm failed to re-establish itself successfully here, although it was to do so on Westhay island. This must have been due to a combination of different bedrock, different soils and different land use by the early farmers of the Levels.

Other evidence for the dryland forest is provided by the wood of the trackway. Each piece is identified to species, and the results from three *fig. 10* excavated stretches along the track line are set out in the table below.

TABLE 1   Wood from three Sweet Track areas

	hazel	ash	holly	willow	poplar	oak	alder	elm	dogwood	ivy	birch	apple	lime
South (Cover & Drove)	305	103	87	2	0	204	9	28	0	0	2	4	20
Central (Quag)	121	15	6	0	0	41	0	21	1	0	7	0	34
Central/North (Turbary)	354	45	0	99	40	203	6	15	7	1	15	0	0
Total number of pieces	780	163	93	101	40	448	15	64	8	1	24	4	54

The pattern is one of mixed forest, with oak, elm, lime and ash as the common large trees, hazel and holly for undergrowth, and alder, willow and poplar on the wetter fringes. Lime and ash are relatively common from the Post Track in the southern sites, and the large lime planks provide ample confirmation that this tree was flourishing locally. This is important, because the pollen of lime is never very abundantly represented in pollen diagrams of the Neolithic period. The species was long thought to be relatively scarce in Britain, but Greig and Rackham have now independently suggested that it was a common tree, at least as common as oak, and the Levels wood confirms its presence as a strong-growing tree. It is also tempting to suggest, on a local scale, a correlation between the drop in lime pollen near the Shapwick burtle and the use of lime in the southern half of the track, which contrasts with the northern half where lime pollen is unaffected at the time of track building, and no lime wood has yet been found.

The pieces of wood can also indicate the nature of tree-growth. The lime trunks that were used to make very long, straight planks were from well-

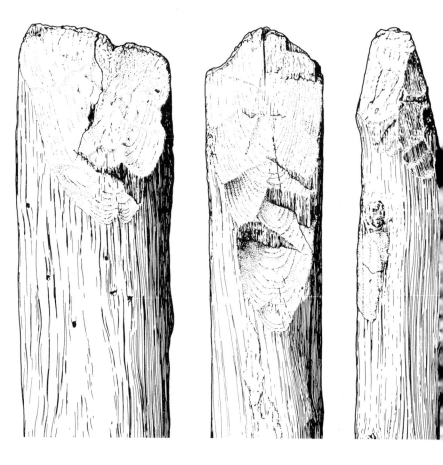

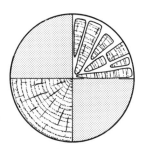

Radial

Tangential

11 Diagram to show the most common methods of splitting an oak trunk into planks.

grown trees, tall and straight and with no low side branches. They had grown in dense forest, competing with other trees for light, but with ample water, warmth and nutrients ensuring strong growth. Some of the oak must have been even more impressive – to judge by the planks we have found – with trunks as tall and straight as the lime, up to 5 m long and up to 1 m in diameter. It is salutary to remember that these trees were felled by people who had no saws of any kind, let alone petrol-driven ones, and no metal tools. The peg wood is often long and straight, perhaps 1 to 1.5 m long and 40–50 mm in diameter, and with little sign of forks or branches such as one finds with top-wood. This is particularly true of the hazel and ash pegs, and these were probably cut from the mass of shoots that spring out from the stool of a felled tree. When deliberately produced, the system is known as coppicing (chapter 5 discusses the evidence further), but a similar result is achieved by forest clearance if the live stumps are left in the ground. More will be said of tree-growth when discussing the tree-ring analyses of Sweet Track wood.

If we marvel at people felling forest giants with stone axes, the detail of their woodmanship is no less impressive. Oak, ash and lime were the main species used to make planks, with oak undoubtedly the preferred species for the walkway. The trunks were converted into planks by splitting with wedges, either of stone or of seasoned oak, and the majority of splits were radial,

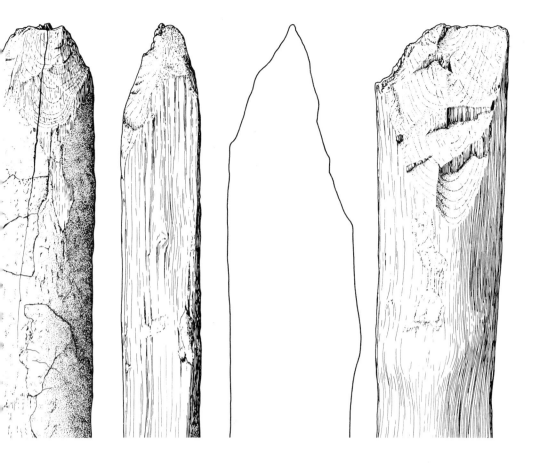

12 *Lower ends of pegs from the Sweet Track, with well-preserved facets left by a stone axe or flint axe. The righthand peg is also shown in section to illustrate the profile of a typical wedge end. Wood species from left to right: hazel, unident., hazel, holly, unident., hazel. Scale 1:2.*

exploiting the tendency of oak to split along its rays. Some, called tangentials, were produced by splitting at right angles to the rays, more or less around the rings, and some by splitting diagonally across the trunk. These more difficult splits were used for the smaller oak trunks, where radial planks would have been rather narrow (only half the diameter of the trunk).

Many of the planks were then holed or notched. The holes were cut through by axing from both plank surfaces, and the readiness of oak to split along its rays was once again turned to account: the axe was used only to cut through the plank thickness across the grain, and then the sides of the hole parallel to the plank sides were wedged out. plate 26

The lower ends of pegs bear many signs of axing, and the facets are often extremely well-preserved, because the pegs were driven into the wet, protective peat very soon after they had been sharpened to a point. Some of the ends are illustrated in fig. 12 and the clarity of the facets indicates that a sharp blade was wielded with precision. Occasionally, the fatter poles were split in plate 25 half or quarters before sharpening, and, in some stretches of the track, pegs were made from oak planking, possibly timbers surplus to requirements for the walkway. The illustrations will convey as well as words can do the quality of Neolithic woodworking, and the wealth of well-preserved evidence which the Sweet Track provides. The contrast with dryland sites is great, and the Sweet evidence becomes all the more important when one considers the role of wood in early technologies, and how rarely it survives at all on most sites, let alone in a state which makes detailed studies possible.

Tree-ring studies

Survival of such a quantity of wood has also encouraged the development of tree-ring analyses. Ruth Morgan first came to the Levels as a volunteer digger on the Sweet Track in 1972 and she has been closely connected with our work ever since, specializing in the tree-ring analyses of wood from many structures. When she began work on samples from the Sweet Track, she was concerned primarily with building up a floating oak tree-ring chronology and samples from the Railway Site made it possible to build up a 314-year mean curve for oak. Ash, hazel and alder were also examined, and the range of species was further increased when the Drove Site was excavated in 1977. By 1981, with the excavation of the Turbary Site, virtually every piece of wood was being sampled for tree-ring analysis, including one or two which were to be conserved whole, and for these the sample was returned after the rings had been measured.

Colour plates (*pages 53, 54*)

X The Eclipse hurdle trackway, seen here just south of Meare island. The second-millennium bc hurdles were woven largely from hazel. The peat cuts beyond have destroyed most of the track.

XI The Walton Heath hurdle track, *c.*2300 bc. This part of the line was soft and wet, and the builders dumped many hurdles, some broken, onto the patch before placing the track hurdles on top. The structure had been damaged by peat-cutting about thirty-to-fifty years previously, and the signs of old peat trenches are angular and clear.

XII, XIII Conservation of wood from the Levels. These S.E.M. photographs show the intact structure of fresh oak (left) and the several degraded and distorted structures of Sweet Track oak (right). The conservation process has to be adapted to cope with such internal collapse.

XI

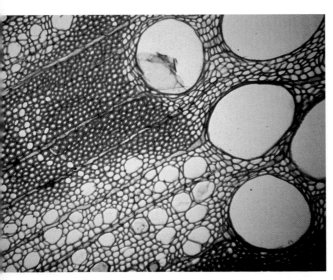

XII

 XIII

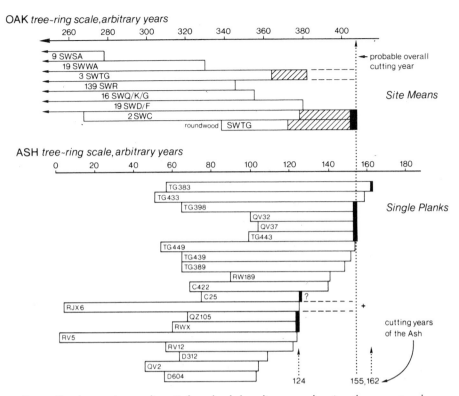

OAK *tree-ring scale, arbitrary years*

13 *Sweet Track tree-ring studies. Oak and ash bar diagrams showing the correspondence of cutting years. Sapwood is shaded, and the solid black line represents bark edges. The ash shows a few pieces cut, for repairs, after the main building year, and some ash was felled thirty-one years before the track-building year, e.g. QZ 105 and RWX.*

The many oak samples examined now provide a mean curve 410 years long, which has been cross-matched with the ash mean curve. In the 1970s, no oak sapwood was found and this meant that the year of felling could not be established. The sapwood of oak is prone to rot, and Neolithic woodworkers had trimmed it off, lengthening the life of their planks but reducing the precision of tree-ring studies! The method of construction of the track meant that plank sides had to be strong, wedged as they were in the peg crossings, and sapwood would soon have rotted and therefore caused the planks to slip. In 1981, oak sapwood was found on young roundwood pegs and three planks from the Turbary Site, which could be matched to the mean curve, and the match was confirmed the following year by one piece of oak with complete sapwood from the Cover Site to the south. It was now possible for Morgan to demonstrate that most of the oak and much of the ash found along the whole length of the Sweet Track had been felled in the same year. This indicated that the track had been built in a single year, constituting a major event in the life of the Neolithic community during that year. Some ash was felled seven years or

fig. 13

so later than the building-year of the Sweet Track, and was made into planks which were used at the Turbary Site, in the particularly wet area discussed above; the original structure, though strengthened here at the time of building, had needed repairs and reinforcement after a few years' use and weathering. On the other hand, a few ash planks had been felled three decades before the track was built; their use in the interim period is something of a puzzle, but their early felling date is evidence for people in the area a generation before the year of track-building.

Morgan has also established a hazel mean curve, and it too shows most pieces felled in one year, and some cut up to ten years later: presumably to mend damaged areas. The tree-ring evidence for repairs gives us the best indicator yet of the length of time the Sweet Track was in use: at least ten years, to judge by the hazel repairs, but probably little longer since neither oak nor ash nor hazel was felled and added to the trackway more than a decade from the year of building. When the Sweet Track was first seen in 1970, we little expected such close dating of events that took place some 6000 years ago.

The tree-ring analyses inform us on many other aspects of track construction and tree-growth, more than we can consider in detail here. But we should note that the hazel samples indicate the possibility of a seven-year coppice cycle, which would suggest deliberate forest management rather than fortuitous growth from the stumps of trees felled for other reasons. And a fascinating picture has begun to emerge, showing the differences in the woodlands exploited to build the southern end of the trackway, compared with those used to build the rest of it. From the northern terminal all the way to the southern edge of the Nature Reserve, large oaks up to 400 years old were used for planking, but for the southern 200 m of the track, immature oak trees were used, little over a century old. The hazel wood also falls into two patterns, consisting roughly of a northern and a southern group, though these are not as clearly separated as in the case of the oak. Variations in the species identified along the line have also been noted, with, for example, holly found only to the south and poplar to the north. The picture is far from complete, but the evidence does allow us to create a realistic reconstruction of the variations present in the Neolithic forests, to set beside the sweeping generalization of 'mixed oak woodland' so often put forward for southern Britain in the Neolithic. It also suggests that by the late fourth millennium bc forest stands were already of varying ages, and not all primary, untouched forest. Moreover, the southern oak trees had started growing only a century or so before they were felled; there was presumably clear ground, therefore, on the burtle or the Polden slopes for them to grow on, yet no forest disturbance shows up for this time on the southern pollen diagrams. It is a reminder of how much past activity must go undetected in the normal course of events.

Sweet artifacts

When we turn to the artifacts found beside the trackway, and to material such as flint, one might expect the range of evidence to be similar to that from dryland sites. After all, flint does not decay for lack of water. But the peat has once again sealed and protected slender threads of evidence which rarely survive elsewhere. Flint artifacts have been found on almost all the major sites excavated. Arrowheads come from the southern sites only; five were carefully made leaf-shaped arrowheads, and one a well-struck flake. The number is low compared with the hundreds found on some Neolithic sites, such as Carn Brea in Cornwall, but of these six arrowheads, two were attached to fragmentary hazel shafts and a third had a lump of black sticky material left on it, presumably the glue which once held it to its shaft. One of the arrowheads had been bound to its hazel shaft by nettle-fibre thread.

plate 27

The function of arrowheads is fairly obvious, to shoot man or beast, and we wonder if their concentration towards the south end of the track implies that this is where the targets were to be found. The function of flint flakes is less immediately obvious, and on many dryland sites rich in flint, unretouched flakes of indeterminate shape are accorded little attention, especially when they carry cortex, as a number of the Sweet Track ones do. But Graeme Morris, in his research on use-wear analysis, realized the potential of these flakes, dropped in the wet marsh and protected by the developing peat from all disturbance. It is not often that we can be sure that no one, in antiquity or at a later time, has trodden on or otherwise damaged a discarded flake. By examining the Sweet Track flints under the microscope, Morris has been able to show that at least two distinct types occur. The first are flakes with a natural cortex back, and were used to cut wood. The second rarely have any cortex, tend to be longer than the woodworking flakes, and were used to cut reeds. A third group of quite short flakes probably exists; we have yet to establish their function but the majority of them are smeared with a rainbow-coloured deposit, which occurs on or near the utilized edges of the flakes. Further magnification has identified the rainbow deposit as fibrous plant material, so this third group of flakes was used to cut plants, probably not reeds, but quite what is not yet known. There was also one broken flake that had been used to cut hide. Looking at the distribution of the different types of flakes, woodworking ones are more common near the southern end of the trackway, and reed-cutting ones near the central stretch. There may be some correlation here with the vegetation around the trackway, when one remembers the evidence for increased wetness at the Turbary Site and therefore more reeds and less fenwood.

fig. 14

A further glimpse of Neolithic habits is provided by the discovery of a small flint core at the Turbary Site. Three flakes had been struck from it shortly before it was dropped, indicating that someone may have carried it around and struck off a new flake whenever he needed a fresh cutting edge. In time, a core

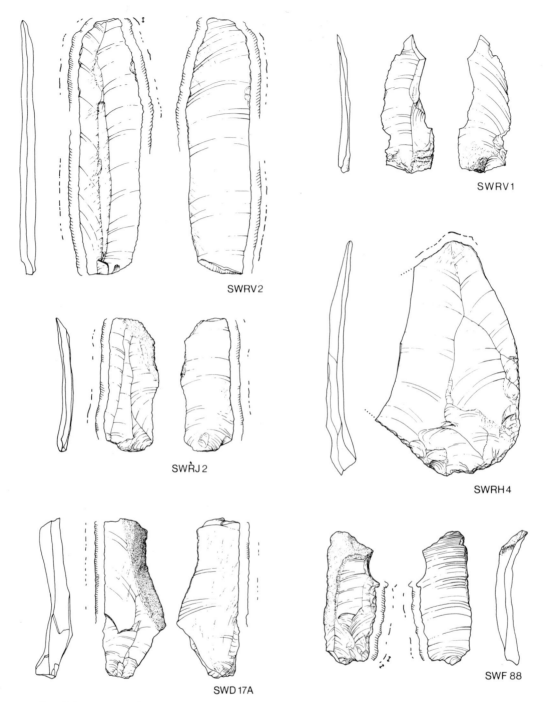

SWRV 1

SWRV 2

SWRJ 2

SWRH 4

SWD 17A

SWF 88

14 Flint flakes associated with the Sweet Track. Most of the flakes were used as tools; the hatched and broken lines and arrows indicate different types of wear and damage to the flake edges. SWD 17A and SWF 88 were woodworking tools, SWRV 2 and SWRJ 2 were reed-cutting tools. SWRH 4 was used for hide-cutting. SWRV 1 was unused. Scale 1:1.

needs re-shaping by the removal of a core-rejuvenation flake, and the discovery of one such flake from the Factory Site supports this view that cores were taken to wherever the work was in progress.

Flint was used for axes as well as for small flakes. One was found lying beside the trackway at the Factory Site. It looked quite unused, but we suppose it to be of the type that was needed to cut rails and pegs to length. The flint has been tentatively identified by a British Museum research team as coming from one of the Sussex mines, a long walk from the Levels. A second axe, found on Meare Heath far from any known Neolithic structure, may have come from the same source as the Sweet specimen, for it was virtually identical in colour, shape and weight.

plate 28

The flint axes, so obviously imported from a distance, remind us that the flakes were also not of local origin. Contact is thus implied with areas beyond the immediate region, and confirmed by a dramatic discovery at the Railway Site, approximately midway along the track. Here, in 1973, one of the volunteers announced that she had found something pale and shiny, a bit like shell, poking out from beneath a piece of split oak. The peat was cleared further, and the material seen to be a green stone, not shell. It looked like the corner of an axe blade, and we thought that it was probably a broken blade, though we hoped otherwise. Our hopes were realized when the oak board was lifted and we saw a perfect, slender, polished green blade. It was an object of great beauty, and immediately two questions sprang to mind: why was there no haft and how had the axe blade come to be left in the marsh beside the trackway? The unusual character of the find has been underlined by the British Museum identification of the stone as jadeite, probably from a source in the Alpine foothills: a sea journey and many hundreds of kilometres from the Levels. At the time of discovery, very few jade axes were known in Britain other than as stray finds, and the date of this type of blade was most uncertain. It could well have been Early Bronze Age but the Sweet discovery showed one at least to have been brought to Britain much earlier than expected, in the early centuries of the Neolithic. Research on the jade axes has indicated that some were functional as axes and others possibly ceremonial, and the Sweet Track axe falls into the latter category. This makes us think that it may have been deliberately put beside the track, rather than accidentally lost, although our own experience of building a track and tramping around in sloppy, wet marshes, feet entangled in a muddy network of rhizomes and decayed reeds, has brought home to us how easy it would be to lose an axe for good, once it had been dropped (chapter 5).

plate 29

plate VIII

Pottery was dropped along the trackway, presumably by people using the path to cross the marsh, unlike the flint which may have been discarded by the builders. The pots were usually greyish in colour, well-made, with fine, smooth walls, a rounded base, marked carination and everted rim; no coarse pottery has been found. Sometimes, almost complete pots were recovered, including one with a wooden stirrer or spurtle beside it, and one that had been

fig. 15
plate 30

15 Reconstruction drawing of the clay pots found beside the Sweet Track. Typical of the earlier Neolithic, they have rounded bases, and a distinct carination, but no decoration other than a burnished black slip.

full of hazel nuts when dropped. Isobel Smith has examined much of the pottery, and found some to have been coated with a black colouring material and then burnished to a shiny, slightly faceted finish. This was a technique used by the far south-western potters, whose gabbroic wares were common at Carn Brea in Cornwall and reached Hembury in Devon at a time close to that of the Sweet Track. The Sweet pottery is not made of the south-western gabbroic clay, however, despite the similarities of shape and black painting. This was an unexpected discovery, given the known wide distribution in the south west of gabbroic pots, and the Sweet builders' ability to import other materials, namely flint and jade.

Wooden artifacts found beside the trackway provide the main evidence from southern Britain for the Neolithic tools and weapons which must so commonly have been made from organic materials. Some are expected types, things which we know people needed and which could only have been made of wood, such as bows to accompany the arrowheads. Four possible bows have been found, three of them near the southern end where most arrowheads were discovered. Made of hazel, and all of them broken, they seem to have been fairly roughly constructed, unlike the fine yew specimen recovered from Meare Heath and dated a few centuries later than the Sweet Track. One from the Turbary Site was only about 1 m long and may have been a child's bow. Another child's toy is a small wooden tomahawk found at the Drove Site and *fig. 16* consisting of two slats of oak fitted together to make something resembling a hafted stone axe. Otherwise, there are no axe hafts, though several possible handles for flint blades have been found.

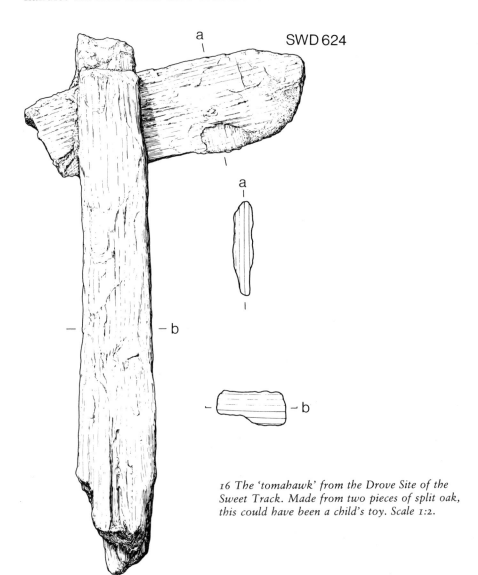

16 *The 'tomahawk' from the Drove Site of the Sweet Track. Made from two pieces of split oak, this could have been a child's toy. Scale 1:2.*

Many of the wooden objects are of uncertain function. Three were shaped like paddles or spades, and it is more likely that they were used to propel a boat than to dig a hole, given their watery context and the slenderness of the blades. The list of wooden artifacts is long and varied, and it includes digging sticks, a probable mattock, toggles, points, a comb, and burnt fragments of the bowl of a spoon. One wooden container has been found, a hollowed-out piece of oak just over 20 cm long; the outside is fairly rough but the inside was once carefully shaped, and the outline is not unlike that of the flint axe blade from the same site. Perhaps this was a wooden box with a lid, designed to hold the axe, and the whole assemblage was dropped, burst apart and lost when the owner slipped on a wet plank. The axe was found to one side of the track, and the container only 4 m to the south and on the other side, so a relationship between the two is certainly possible. If blades were boxed for travel it would account for the perfect condition of this specimen and for the absence of a haft. The same would apply to the jadeite blade.

plate 32

Personal adornment may have been the purpose of wooden artifacts of another type found beside the Sweet Track. These are carefully shaped, slender rods or pins of yew, split out of a branch and whittled and polished to a round section at one end and tapering to a point at the other. They were found curved, but have tended to straighten in the course of conservation; we assume that they were meant to be curved, and were steamed and bent to the required shape, but they may simply have bent on becoming waterlogged, as split pieces of wood tend to do. The shortest pin was a mere 160 mm long, and slightly expanded just before the tip; the longest was 276 mm, and tapered evenly to a fine point, as did the other two finished specimens. The fifth pin, which seemed to have been lost in the course of manufacture, was still squarish in section, blunt and barely beginning to taper. We have enjoyed some lengthy speculation about the possible function of these pins: as nose, hair or infibulation pins, cloak, bag or tent fasteners, netting needles, eating sticks or wooden arrowtips. The yew wood may have been selected for its colour, or for the strength and flexibility which makes it so suitable for bows and which would have been useful in a fastening pin. The only comparable objects from the British Neolithic are the bone pins found with some later Neolithic burials, at Dorchester and at Stonehenge for example, where the context of discovery suggests that they could have fastened together a bag which held the cremated remains of the deceased. We are not suggesting burials along the Sweet Track, although it is true that nothing would remain in the peat of leather bag or burnt bone and the only trace would be exactly what we did find, a wooden pin.

plate 31

The track-builders

All told, a wealth of evidence from the Sweet Track points to the activity of people in the area, and sometimes illuminates a particular event with unusual clarity. But we do not know where people lived, nor the size of their settlements, because they had more sense than to live in the marsh, where evidence would have survived for us. From time to time in our investigations, however, there is a slight clue as to the nature and location of the Sweet Track builders' homes.

The tree-ring evidence indicates that the bulk of the wood for the trackway was felled in one year, both big trees for planks and slender ones for rails; and the poles for pegs were cut at the same time. Conversion of trunks into planks must have been immediate, because the roundwood in the structure (pegs and rails) was cut to length and sharpened on site before it seasoned. It was a matter of weeks, not years, for the track components to be assembled ready for building, and at a rough estimate there was enough wood for 6000 pegs, 2000 m of rails (500 young trees?) and over 4000 m of planking. Over a dozen different species of tree had been felled, from two different areas of woodland: a northern one with large, old oaks and a southern one with much younger oak trees. The planks had been split and holed on dry-land (although notches were cut on site) and the roundwood was cut into manageable lengths. This was work for more than two families, given that it was executed quickly, and in two separate areas of woodland. It is likely that there were working groups of at least half a dozen adults, and probably more. Two communities must have existed, a northern and a southern group, not necessarily living in villages but certainly working together when the occasion demanded, as it did for the track-building.

What more do we know of these groups? They had been in the area for a generation at least, in all likelihood, since a system of woodland management may have been established for a quarter of a century or so (as hazel tree-ring evidence shows) and a little of the ash wood had been felled thirty-one years before the track was built. They stayed for another ten years, since the trackway was repaired during the decade following building. They may have stayed longer, of course, but their track was lost to sight in the decaying marsh vegetation that was soon to engulf the structure in its protective peat covering.

These people were probably farmers, but it is worth noting that the evidence for the association of the track-builders with agriculture is slight, consisting of some cereal-type pollen, coming probably from Westhay island, and pollen evidence for forest clearance and an influx of weeds, usually associated with growing crops and grazing animals. The material culture found beside the trackway, the pottery, arrowheads and axe blades, is similar to that from other early Neolithic sites where cereal grains and the bones of domestic animals have been found. But no direct evidence has been found to indicate that the track-builders and users were farmers. They were certainly hunters, using their bows and arrows to good effect, and no doubt the full range of local resources was exploited, including fish and birds as well as mammals, and plants in abundance. We say this because the people who built and used the trackway were clearly affluent, in the sense that they had access to fine pottery, and to good quality flint which had to be imported, and that someone who walked along the trackway had acquired a very beautiful jadeite axe blade.

External contacts existed, therefore, as well as the local ones implied by the very presence of the trackway, but it is not easy to relate this precisely dated structure to the Early Neolithic sites and artifacts of the region. Many stone and flint axes, and quantities of flakes and cores, are known on the Mendips north of the Levels, and it is tempting to posit a relationship between the funerary and settlement activities on the hills, and the making and using of the Sweet Track. But the dating of the upland material is very imprecise, and we think it illogical to draw comparisons or suggest intimate connections. Nonetheless, the 100 flint arrowheads, and stone axes, from Quaking House on the Quantocks to the south-west, and the abundant arrowheads and axes from Ham Hill in south-eastern Sedgemoor, indicate the importance of such flint artifacts to Neolithic people, in their hunting (and perhaps warfare) and woodworking. A few further comments on external relations are made in chapter 4, but by any criteria, the Sweet Track is a unique artifact and an important addition to our evidence for Early Neolithic Britain.

Finally, a comment on the time taken to build the trackway. Our experimental reconstruction (chapter 5) showed that building was the least of the tasks, compared to the arduous work of felling, preparing and transporting the wood to site. We suggest that once all timber and roundwood was on the site, two groups of at least half a dozen adults each could have built the Sweet Track in a day's work.

4 Establishing the network: tracks of the Neolithic

> Where a tribe was quite populous, with well-established villages, then a few paths would gradually become well-used, even maintained, linking one community with another . . .
>
> (J. Coles)

During the millennium from the time of the Sweet Track to the end of the Neolithic, the wet areas of the Levels changed considerably. Where there had been flat swathes of reeds and sedges with no more than an occasional tree, there was now a spreading fenwood, and large patches of willow, birch and alder flourished in the wetlands. As the trees died and collapsed into the water, *plate* their rotting remains helped to build up the ground level. Within a few *III* centuries, the higher spots were above the general water-table and fed only by rainwater. In these areas, a raised bog of *Sphagnum* moss, heather and cotton-grass began to grow: in comparison with reed swamps, a squashy, acid and impoverished environment. Yet some areas stayed covered by reeds or fenwood, and the wetlands of the Levels supported a more diverse range of habitats at the end of the Neolithic than at the beginning.

The record of dryland changes, preserved in the peats along with the plants and pollen of the wetland, was for Harry Godwin one of the great attractions of work in the Levels. Here was the raw material for his major research project in the post-glacial history of the British vegetation, as well as for his more detailed work in the Levels themselves. Yet, however exciting the palaeobotany, Godwin did not neglect the archaeological evidence preserved in the peat. He was a firm advocate of the value of combined environmental and archaeological studies, although he obviously had his doubts about some archaeologists' commitment when he wrote 'I fancy that many an archaeologist at heart prefers the dry chalk trench to the soaking black peat face.' He himself published a number of papers which combined the two approaches to the past, and much of his work is published in the *Proceedings of the Prehistoric Society* for 1960. Here he related Neolithic and Bronze Age episodes of track-building to changes in both local and wider environmental conditions. Subsequent work has modified this interpretation in that new discoveries have been made of structures built at other times, but Godwin's general outline of wetland and dryland vegetation remains largely unchanged.

Radiocarbon Calibration

0 bc	0 BC
500	500
	1000
1000	
	1500
1500	2000
2000	2500
	3000
2500	
	3500
3000	
	4000
	CALIBRATED
3500	
UNCALIBRATED	

The filling-in of the detail was begun by Alan Hibbert and continued by the Project environmentalists Stephen Beckett and Astrid Caseldine. Hibbert, for example, worked on the variation in contemporary pollen deposits in different parts of the Levels and in 1973 published a transect of pollen diagrams which indicated where Neolithic farmers had preferred to fell the forest and make their fields (see chapter 3). In 1979, Beckett and Hibbert published the results of their intensive studies of pollen influx rates and comparisons of deep monoliths from different parts of the Levels. They concluded that it was possible to distinguish a sequence of regional pollen zones from about 3500 bc when peat formation started, to about ad 500.

The sequence begins in the mid-fourth millennium, a time when we suspect people were living in the Levels and on the sandy burtle islands, although we have no direct evidence. Clues are provided by the many Mesolithic flints, some of which could have been abandoned in the centuries after 4000 bc; there is also the Sweet Track tree-ring evidence for possible episodes of early forest clearance, discussed in chapter 3. But the pollen record itself gives no indication of human presence, and from 3500 bc to the time of the Sweet Track – the period of regional Pollen Zone A – the dryland was covered with a forest

fig. 17

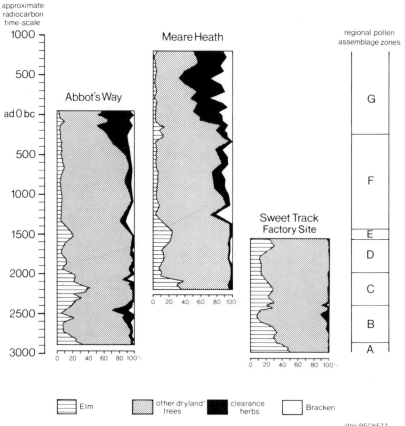

17 *Pollen zones in the Somerset Levels. The zones A–G represent the major phases in the development of regional vegetation, emphasizing the relative importance of forest cover, open ground and plants associated with farming.*

after BECKETT

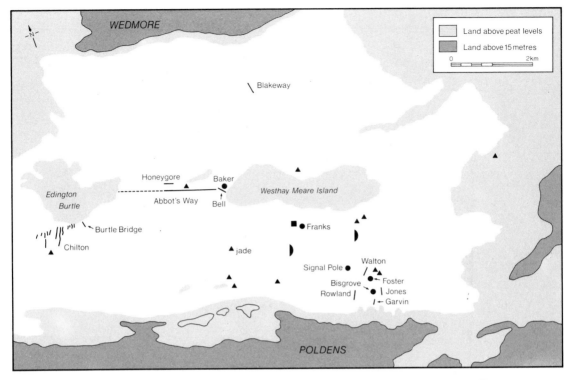

▲ axe
❭ bow
■ mallet

18 Later Neolithic trackways, platforms and stray finds from the Brue valley. Also included are the two Sweet axes.

dominated by elm, oak and lime. The building of the Sweet Track seems to mark the opening of a new phase, Zone B, when the forest cover was partially cleared, and pollen values of elm and then lime decline. Increases in weed pollen suggest that this clearance was for farming, and that the opening of the forest lasted for 400 years, if not more. In the following Zone C, elm pollen increases along with that of other trees, and grasses decrease. This pattern reflects a regeneration of forest cover, which lasted until the late third millennium bc. Judging by the pollen evidence, the woods of the late Neolithic differed from those available to the earliest farmers, with, for example, more ash, less lime, and an absence of elm on the sandy Shapwick burtle. The archaeological evidence discussed in this chapter spans the later part of Zone B, Zone C and the opening of Zone D, a phase of minor clearance.

Two areas within the Levels have proved particularly rich in later Neolithic evidence. One lies to the east, and just north of the Polden Hills, an area now known as Walton Heath where intensive peat-cutting has revealed a number of trackways leading out from the hills, near a freshwater spring. We can envisage farming settlements here, and people setting off to cross the reedy

fig. 18

swamp, perhaps wanting to reach the Meare-Westhay island that lay in the middle of the wetland. As the centuries passed, and reed swamps gave way to fenwood and raised bog, they built different sorts of trackway and often needed only to bridge the soft and soggy lagg that lay between the dryland and the bog, or to fill in a wet and dangerous patch on their way across to Meare.

The second area with a concentration of Neolithic evidence is also a departure point: the edge of the Meare-Westhay island close to the present village of Westhay. The people travelling from here were heading west, towards Edington Burtle, which is the largest sand island in the valley. From 2800 to 2000 bc this was a popular route, and one where a continuous built road seems to have been more necessary than across Walton Heath, for we have traced several tracks for hundreds of metres. The Honeygore track, built

plate XIV   c. 2800 bc, crossed wet fenwood, whereas the Abbot's Way of c. 2000 bc crossed spongy raised bog, yet we suspect that both ran from island to island.

From the southern edge of Edington Burtle, the Chilton Heath tracks run to the Poldens, aiming for the Butterwell valley, some 8.5 km west of the routes leading on to Walton Heath. In c. 2400 bc, therefore, people could have walked from home on the Poldens north along the Garvin's trackway to Meare-Westhay island, west along the island and on along the Honeygore track to Edington Burtle, across the burtle and south to the Poldens using the Chilton Heath brushwood trackways, then eastwards home along the slopes of the hills. The round trip was about 22 km long, and slightly under a half of it was on prepared routes across wet ground.

The tour is hypothetical, of course. We cannot be sure that any Neolithic individual ever walked this route. But we do know that many of them used the different sections of it across the centuries, and we can reconstruct some of the landscape that they observed in passing, as well as those areas where they farmed and hunted and managed the woodlands. We also know of one of the mammals they encountered, as we shall see below.

The outline of the third millennium bc in the Levels has been gradually built up, in ways that typify the work of the Project. In this chapter, we shall examine some of the more significant approaches beginning with the job of the Field Archaeologist, whose steady field-work over the years has made it possible for us to reconstruct the outline of Neolithic activity on Walton Heath.

Field-work in the Levels

Field-work on the moors and in the peat-cuts is not something new to the Project. In chapter 2 we saw how Bulleid and Dewar devoted their spare time to the archaeology of the peats, and University-based work began with Godwin in the 1940s and has been continued by us. This has set the pattern for field-work in the Levels, a mixture of walking endless peat-cuts, vaulting bottomless ditches, eyeing pasture fields for humps and bumps and exploiting

G WALTON II   ST 45293930

WALTON HEATH   FISONS
                   MACHINE CUT, EAST— WEST HEADS.

Pre–1978 info on a previous card.
Walton track now removed apart from in
drove at S. of field.
Cut July, 78. Walked July 1978. CA+CRS. SFno. 78.29. wood pieces.
Partly cut October 78 Report 24.10.78 CRS   Finished. Report 8·12·78.
{ Decad SF 78.64, 65, 66, Single poles & a group of ash timbers in Heads 11, 14, 18. }
{ Plan brought up to date 7/12/78 CRS   Area Report 6-2-79
Cut & Walked. July/Aug '79. Completed } 17·8·79. Plan brought up to date KRC.
79·39, 79·42, 79·43 (all wood).   reported
Cutting, end Sept — 13·10·79. S most 19 heads & 3 most N. ones. Walked. KRC.
Cutting Heads 20 – 33 , 26·11·79 – 4·12·79. Walked, KRC   Area Report Dec 79
Cutting Sept : S. end in prs (Higher), N. end in singles. SF 80·29. (stemwood)
   "   Oct; N. end opp heads, 6·10·80, KRC   Area Report 17·12·80

Walked 9/81. RPC SF.81.23. & KRC   4·10·81.
30 heads walked 27/7/82. CJS   SF. 8241
~~No heads walked 76 83 And~~ hauling AW
Unrieldling taking place   16:8:83 SDL.
14 heads walked   31:8:83 SDL. (Hurdle paced in, + head no. 9 from SW)
Hurdle?! Excavated   5/6 Sept '83. SDL, SWB, NACH. ACC.
REMAINING HEADS WALKED (22). 27/9/83 NACH
Walked on 3rd. + 4th. April 84. 36 heads. G.B.O'H.
6 heads cut & walked 29/8/84 SW
A further 31 heads walked. (finished ·14·9·84). G.B.O'H.

19 *Examples of field-recording. A card is kept for every field, and filled in after each visit.*

the best source of all, the people who live and work on the moors, and who discover the majority of the evidence. The Project's present Field Archaeologist would find much that was familiar in Bulleid's discovery of the Meare Iron Age settlement through a sequence of events that included ditch cleaning, bumps in a field emphasized by the haystacks set on them (or their modern alternative of drinking troughs), and a farmer's collection of sherds and other bits and pieces.

The context of field-work is new, however, in that a permanent Field Archaeologist has been employed in the Levels since Department of the Environment funding began in 1973. On the whole, the post has been filled by recent graduates who have worked for a year or so, perhaps combining field-work with a post-excavation project, and then gone on to postgraduate studies or some other more permanent job. They have generally had assistants for the summer months when peat-cutting speeds up and a number of small sites may be excavated. But the permanent Field Archaeologist must be out in the Levels at all times of the year, walking the peat-cuts in summer dust or winter snow and keeping meticulous records in howling gales and sheets of horizontal rain as well as during those glorious days of late spring, when the varied greens are speckled with yellow flag iris and other flowers, orchids appear but have yet to burst their buds, and plovers nest on the exposed peat surfaces of abandoned cutting areas.

Record-keeping can take up as much time as field-walking. There is a card for every field in the Levels, to be filled in after each visit; in this way successive Field Archaeologists can easily check on previous discoveries in a field, and on *fig. 19* the rate of peat-cutting or whatever else may be going on (almost). Every find is given a number, and a card is filled out with details of location, peat-type,

---

Colour plates (*pages 71, 72*)

XIV The Abbot's Way, a corduroy road of the Late Neolithic, made largely of split alder logs.

XV A selection of small finds from Meare Village East, excavated by Bulleid and Gray. Predominantly domestic, the finds include a weaving comb, antler toggles, spindle-whorl, metal blades and a Neolithic flint arrowhead collected by the Iron Age inhabitants.

XVI Small finds from Meare Village West, excavated by the Somerset Levels Project in 1979. Note the diversity of materials from one small area at the edge of the settlement: iron, lead, bronze, tin, glass, bone, antler, shale, and stone.

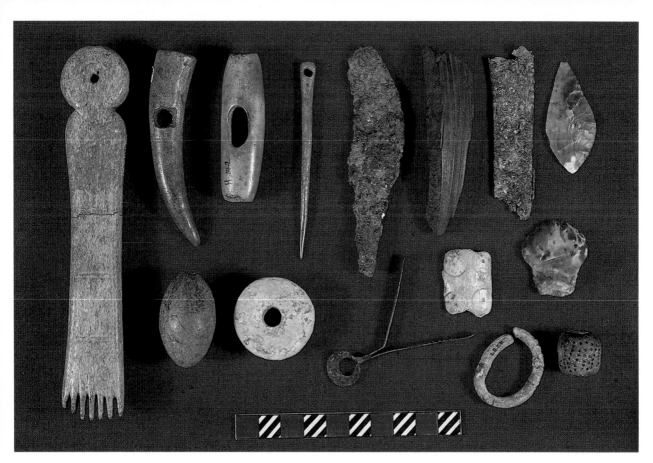

XV XVI

description of the find, details of treatment, etc. Day-books are kept, and at the end of every week, the Field Archaeologist writes a detailed report of work done. In due course, these records are summarized by area and form the background for our understanding of past human activity throughout the Levels, pointing to those spots where virtually nothing has ever been found (e.g. Godney Moor) as well as to those where repeated finds over the years indicate a route or an activity even though no built trackway or structure has been encountered. These records provide an essential complement to the more obvious evidence revealed by the excavation of built trackways, and their value should not be underestimated.

Discoveries are not common, and walking the peat-cuts can be as monotonous as pacing up and down a ploughed field. But field-work in the Levels is enlivened by a variety of local hazards, such as the dogs which love to chase a cyclist, or the large Hereford bulls which lurk hidden in a herd of Friesian milk cows until the unwary walker is half way across the field. Both can be escaped by jumping ditches as Godwin did, but one never knows quite how wide and how deep the ditch is until it is too late.

Because the peat is full of natural wood as well as of the brushwood and timbers of built structures, it is not always easy for the inexperienced field-worker to know if a significant find has been made. In early days we were sometimes caught out by fenwood trees, the truncated roots of which looked like a brushwood trackway in section. On one memorable day in the Project's first year, one 'track' turned into a tree on closer inspection and one 'tree', checked just in passing, turned into the solid brushwood trackway that crosses Walton Heath, which we later called Garvin's after the owner of the peatfield where the discovery was made.

A second trackway on Walton Heath was found using our most successful and rewarding technique of field archaeology in the Levels, namely talking to the people who live and work there. In this instance, the talking took place in one of the local pubs visited by Stephen Coleman in an off-duty moment. He was soon joined by one of the peat-cutters who told him that the machine preparing one of the Walton Heath fields for cutting (a process called unridding) had scraped away the surface debris to reveal sticks of hazel. Prompt inspection the next morning confirmed the presence of 'unnatural' wood in the peat, and excavation by the summer field team soon revealed a fine expanse of hurdle-work. Further field-work and excavation would in due course show this to be a later Neolithic hurdle trackway, the Walton Heath   plate XI
track, and perhaps one of our most important finds.

The discovery of the Walton Heath hurdle trackway was a highlight of field-work. Other finds are more mundane, an occasional flint flake or ash pole for example. But these items were dropped by someone prehistoric as they crossed the bog, and regular field-walking and recording over the years has built up a pattern of past human activity on Walton Heath based on small finds of wood as well as on the discovery of built trackways.

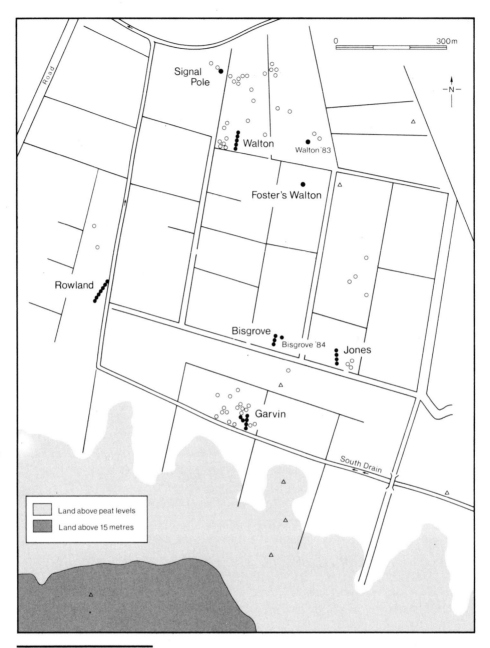

20 *Later Neolithic discoveries from Walton Heath, showing the density of activity in this area. The map is the product of over a decade of field-work.*

The area shown in fig. 20 includes at least thirty peatfields; cutting-rate differs according to owner, type of peat and economic climate, and some have been cut and walked many times, others only once or twice in the years since 1973. Before then, no prehistoric evidence was known from this area of the Levels, a blank both in Godwin's survey published in 1960 and in Coles and Hibbert's Neolithic papers of 1968 and 1970. In late 1973, within a month or so of first having a Field Archaeologist in the Levels, the Garvin's brushwood trackway was discovered. In 1975, the Walton Heath and Rowland's hurdle trackways were found, and in 1979 brushwood bundles turned up near Garvin's and a birch brushwood trackway was found by Caroline Sturdy in Jones' peatfield. In all except the latter case, the peat-cuts had been made at right angles to the track alignments, thereby exposing good sections, sometimes in several successive heads. But the heads in Jones' were aligned north–south, almost parallel to the prehistoric structure, and a long stretch of trackway was removed in a single peat-cut. In 1980, a further brushwood structure was revealed in Bisgrove's field, where the peat was being rotavated.

plate 33

Late the following year, more birch brushwood was found near Rowland's trackway, in a field which members of the Project knew as Singapore. But the discovery of the prehistoric structure by Kay Campbell led to discussion with the peat company about excavation, and she learnt that the name of the field was really Signal Pole, a designation which today looks almost as obscure as Singapore until one remembers the nearby railway line that once ran from Glastonbury to Highbridge.

In 1983, a new small area of hurdle-work was found near the Walton Heath trackway, and in 1984 a brushwood structure similar to Signal Pole turned up in Foster's field, and another at Bisgrove. In addition to these structures, many isolated pieces of wood have been recorded over the years, especially in the vicinity of the Garvin's, Jones' and Walton routes. Near the latter, for example, almost thirty separate finds of worked wood have been made.

Neolithic activity on Walton Heath

Now that the structures have been excavated, and radiocarbon-dated, and palaeoenvironmental analyses have been made of their associated peats, and tree-ring analyses of the individual pieces of wood, it is possible to place them in rough chronological order and environmental context. The earliest surviving evidence for human activity in the area comes from the hurdle-like fragment known as Walton '83 and the heap of birch brushwood at Signal Pole. The former was found near the Walton hurdle trackway, but somewhat lower in the peats, and it was not a true woven hurdle; it has one radiocarbon date of c. 2700 bc. The heap at Signal Pole may be a century later, and not long afterwards the first major structure was built on the eastern side of the area at Jones'. When this brushwood trackway was laid down, a sparse fenwood was growing in the reedy marsh, along with abundant *Cladium*, indicating shallow

21 *Reconstruction drawing of the Garvin's brushwood track, leading out onto the raised bog. Drawn by R. Walker.*

standing water. Pollen evidence for the vegetation cover on the Poldens suggests that the trackway-building took place well within Pollen Zone B, the first notable clearance of forest cover in the region. Signal Pole and Walton '83 would therefore be contemporary with the earlier part of this phase of forest *fig. 21* clearance and the Garvin's brushwood trackway, at about 2400 bc, is associated with peats laid down towards the end of Zone B. The brushwood bundles found in 1979 are contemporary with Garvin's track, according to peat stratigraphy, radiocarbon dates and tree-ring comparisons. They indicate a spread of activity at this point, at a time when the sparse fenwood was being overtaken by raised bog.

The location in time of Walton and Rowland's hurdle trackways is more   plate 34
difficult. Radiocarbon results indicate that they were built at the same time as
Garvin's, or only shortly afterwards. The surface that they crossed was one of
developing raised bog with isolated fenwood and wet patches, similar to
Garvin's. But pollen analysis of the associated peat suggests that the Walton
trackway was built as much later as Zone D, after the local dryland forest had
regenerated. For the moment, we can only say that both Walton and
Rowland's were built in the later third millennium bc, and that they were
possibly contemporary since study of the growth-patterns of the hazel rods
shows them to be very similar. The correlation of radiocarbon dates and
pollen zones is an area for future research, and one that will probably have to
await the calibration of radiocarbon dates against local tree-ring chronologies.

The activity taking place immediately around the two hurdle trackways
seems to have been different, despite their contemporaneity. Or perhaps it
would be more accurate to say that field-walking has produced much evidence
of worked wood to either side of the Walton trackway, and some of this is   fig. 20
contemporary for it is at the same level in the peat. Around Rowland's, by
contrast, field-walking has drawn a blank. We can therefore imagine people
hurrying along the Rowland's hurdles to get where they wanted, but stopping
along the Walton stretch and perhaps wandering off to one side on drier days,
to collect plants or hunt birds, and then continuing on their way across the
bog.

The Neolithic yew bows from Meare Heath and Ashcott Heath, along with
various flint arrowheads, provide ample evidence of the hunting activities of
these people in the rich watery environments. The Meare Heath bow is the   fig. 22
earliest 'English' longbow, capable of casting an arrow over 100 m.   fig. 23

The abundance of arrowheads, and axes, found on Neolithic sites on the
Mendips and Quantocks has already been noted, and here again we are faced
with the difficulty of establishing what relationship existed between the
occupants of the Levels, and those communities living on the Mendips and
Quantocks. We think it unlikely that the trackways and platforms were built
and used by people who lived far away, and we prefer to think that the
network of routes was established and maintained by groups who had their
settlements on the Poldens or the sand islands, where their arable fields,
pasture and woodland could be worked. Our environmental evidence
certainly suggests that these activities were carried out very near the wetland.
That the Levels' inhabitants were aware of events on the uplands, and indeed
their utilization of the Mendips and Quantocks, can now only be confirmed by
programmes of research in these regions, rather than in the Levels, where our
evidence has a precision in chronology and in location of activities which so far
is lacking elsewhere in the region.

Because most of the Neolithic finds on Walton Heath have been made
nearer the Poldens than Meare-Westhay island, we tend to assume that
settlement was on the former, perhaps near the freshwater spring of Bradley

22 *Reconstruction drawing of the Meare Heath bow, as it might have been in use. Drawn by M. Rouillard.*

23 *(opposite) The Meare Heath bow, half a longbow of yew broken at the hand-grip and lost in the peat. The reconstruction drawing shows its probable original appearance, including the decorative binding. Drawn by M. Rouillard.*

stream. Consideration of the major structures shown on the map suggests that most traffic in the earlier centuries may have set off from a point to the east of the spring, along the Jones' trackway for example, and that later the starting point was 500 m or so to the west, heading for the Walton Heath hurdle paths. The ploughed fields in this area of the Poldens are walked whenever possible, and so far flints have been found near the probable eastern terminals. Their absence to the west is not really significant, because the land here is under wood and pasture and not conducive to the discovery of prehistoric evidence. Likewise, the absence of evidence for structures more recent than Walton Heath and Rowland's tracks is not significant in terms of the prehistoric use of the area. We do not know, and will never know, what, if anything, took place on Walton Heath in the second and first millennia bc, because the peat was cut away before anyone took an archaeological interest in the area. The effect is even more pronounced for the Bronze Age of Shapwick Heath, as shown in chapter 6. The other side of the coin is that future peat-cutting should yield more evidence from the earlier Neolithic centuries, and in fact the most recent discoveries have been of older structures (e.g. Walton '83, *c.* 2700 bc). Once the peat is worked out, the discoveries will cease.

Investigations at Westhay

The above picture of Neolithic activity on Walton Heath has been pieced together through walking the peat-cuts over the years, and it points to settlement on the Poldens. At the beginning of this chapter, we noted a second area of intense Neolithic activity, on the western edge of the Meare-Westhay island, leading across Westhay Level. Here, evidence has accrued from both peat-cuts and pasture fields, and pursuit of one trackway or structure has several times led to the discovery of a new one. Such was the case when in 1966 the Abbot's Way (p. 34ff.) was being traced to its eastern terminal on the island. The field being examined belonged to Mr Maurice Bell, and when one of his sons learnt of the object of the exercise, he told of some 'sticks' he had seen a short distance to the north, at the bottom of a hole dug to bury his dog Sally. The archaeologists were given permission to exhume Sally, but she had decayed away in the acid peats, and all that remained of interest in her grave were pieces of worked wood, which later proved to come from a trackway of Neolithic date. This was the structure now known as the Bell trackway. Excavation revealed two superimposed tracks, Bell A and Bell B, and as these were traced up towards the island edge it proved necessary to open up a new site on the other side of a hedge. No track was found, but instead a large platform of branches and split roundwood, now named the Baker Platform after Mr Dennis Baker, the owner of the field (this has led to occasional confusion in print, when people assume Bell-Baker to be a misprint for Bell-Beaker, a confusion compounded by the later third-millennium dates associated with the structures and relating to a period when Bell-Beaker

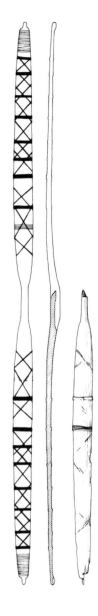

fig. 24

plate 36

plate 35

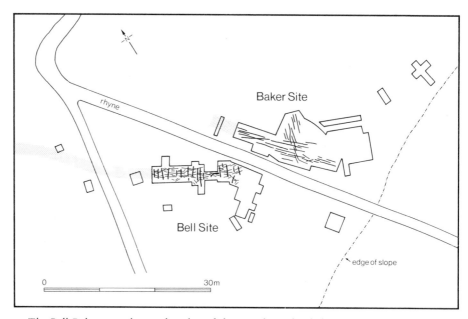

24 *The Bell-Baker complex at the edge of the Westhay island showing excavated areas, main groups of structural timber and main tracks (tone) leading in to the island.*

pottery was current). Excavation of the lower layers of the Platform revealed the terminal of yet another trackway, the Baker track, giving positive evidence for four trackways and one platform where previously only one track was presumed to exist. As the new discoveries all came from pasture fields, it is unlikely that any of them would have been made but for the Abbot's Way tracing. On the other hand, peat-cutting on the moors to the west has yielded another five tracks of third-millennium date, the Honeygore complex.

Excavation of the Bell-Baker complex has produced a diversity of evidence of considerable interest, adding to our understanding of Neolithic activity both in the local context and on a much larger scale. The complex consists of a platform of brushwood, bordered on the north by heavier timbers leading down to a slipway of split alder trunks. To the east, a walkway led up onto the edge of the island. This, the driest part of the structure, was very decayed, but a suggestion of regularity in the alignment of the slight stems points to a tied bundle or perhaps even a woven hurdle. To the west, a brushwood track led out into the marsh. Its surface was much worn, through long exposure or heavy use or perhaps both. The Bell tracks ran up along the southern edge of the Platform; evidence for their exact association with the Platform was destroyed long ago when the hedge and ditch dividing the two fields was made.

The complex must lie very close to a settlement of third-millennium date, and probably one that was occupied for several centuries as the layers of the Platform were built up and the Bell B trackway constructed to replace the earlier Bell A. Radiocarbon dates from wood samples taken from the complex span the entire millennium, placing the slipway at 3000 ± 80 bc and the Bell B track at 2025 ± 92 bc. Tree-ring evidence shows matching growth-patterns for samples from the slipway, the Baker trackway and the lower brushwood platform, and the latter are radiocarbon dated to around 2700–2500 bc. The slipway may therefore not be as old as its one radiocarbon date suggests, but long-term use of the area is still indicated, through phases of forest clearance and regeneration alike (Pollen Zones B–D).

Proximity of settlement is suggested by the concentration of routes leading to the one spot on the shore of Westhay island, and is confirmed by the results of environmental analyses. Grass seeds and other plant remains found on the Platform are from species that would have grown on nearby disturbed ground, such as mallow, dock and dandelion, and swine-cress (*Coronopus squamatus*) which favours trampled places. The beetles associated with the Platform include a relatively high number of dung beetles, which indicate that there were herbivores nearby. These could have been wild deer or other mammals but they could also have been the cattle of Neolithic families living not far from present-day Westhay. One other category of evidence points to the proximity of settlement, namely the discovery of two wooden artifacts associated with the complex. Apart from the Sweet Track, the wooden structures out in the peats have rarely yielded worked objects, and though sparse, the Baker complex finds are rather unusual and not the sort of object, such as bow, arrow or spear, that one might expect to have been lost far from home.

The first to be found was a roughly carved block of ashwood, 16 cm high. It has come to be known as the God-Dolly, a name that reflects the ambiguity of its hermaphroditic appearance, and of its resting place upside-down under the Bell B trackway. Was it a joke? a lost toy? or a carefully deposited ritual object? The second wooden artifact was more prosaic, although its function is again not absolutely clear. It consists of a long piece of oak, with a naturally bent handle at one end and a wide, pointed blade at the other. The blade is worn, and the piece was probably a digging stick or even a simple traction-ard, used in the cultivation of the Westhay slopes.

plate VII

plate 37

Beaver

The above paragraphs outline the evidence for human activity at the Baker complex, and for probable human settlement in the immediate vicinity. Before leaving the site, we must also consider the evidence for construction and settlement by another mammal: the beaver. When we first published the Baker Platform, in 1980, we included two photographs of brushwood ends and wrote that 'the marks of axe or knife on the cut ends were unlike any others from the numerous sites in the Somerset Levels. The technique seems to have been to cut through the branch with a series of closely connected chops or slices, the implement hardly withdrawn from the wood before it cut down again.' Experiments to reproduce the marks were not very successful, and the facets plate 39 could not be satisfactorily duplicated. But within a few months, we had evidence for similar facets being made by beaver. The first suggestion came from a chance remark made by a delegate to the National Maritime Museum Symposium on Woodworking Techniques before AD 1500, where pictures of the Baker wood were shown. Then, drawing the wood for the symposium publication, Sue Rouillard puzzled over the facets, and we chased comparative illustrations and found the best match in a murky colour photo of prehistoric beaver-chewn wood from Denmark, in *Collins' Guide to Animal Tracks and Signs*. Desiring modern comparative pieces to study, we were next directed to Chester Zoo, the nearest establishment housing live beaver, and the Keeper, Mr Wait, kindly sent a few pieces of willow chewed by his charges. The marks of their teeth were identical to the facets on the beaver roundwood. Later in 1981, one of us took a day off from a conservation conference in Ottawa to visit a colony of live beaver in the wild. Here specimens of tooth-marked wood were collected, and observations made of beaver constructions, which led to a reappraisal of the Baker evidence.

First, we noticed that all the multi-faceted wood that had been identified was willow, a species favoured by beaver for food. Secondly, many of the facets had a hard black substance stuck to them, such as is found on bits of wood that beaver have stuck into a dam, or into their underwater winter food store of branches; this substance is mud, not peat. Thirdly, the condition of the prehistoric pieces was very varied, some sharp and fresh and others heavily eroded or weathered. This is typical of the litter of discarded wood that accumulates around a beaver settlement. There was no doubt in our minds, by the autumn of 1981, that some of the wood in the Baker Platform had been felled by beaver, not by humans. It seemed likely that the beaver had built a dam and a lodge in the vicinity before the Platform was built, perhaps giving rise to the increased wetness noted in the environmental samples from slightly below (i.e. before) the Platform level.

plate 40 Our field studies of beaver in 1981 and subsequent years showed us how drastically these animals could affect a landscape, partially through tree-felling but particularly by building their dams, which cause the flooding of many acres in a flat terrain. Given that they were active in the Levels in the Neolithic, around Westhay, we should expect there to have been large expanses of open water held up behind their dams, and it is even possible that they contributed to flooding horizons (chapter 6) and to the formation of Meare Pool, which in medieval years was to be a source of great wealth because of its abundant fish (chapter 7 provides further discussion of Meare Pool).

In the Levels, it is unlikely that beaver had much effect on the up-slope tree cover, given the abundance of marshland habitat and fringing fenwood. But elsewhere, in different terrains where they colonized streams, they could have had an impact equivalent to that postulated for Mesolithic hunters or the earliest farmers, through the removal of enough tree cover to show up on a pollen diagram. By now, we were a long way from the unusual Baker facets, but they were the starting point for a line of reasoning that led to these conclusions, and we can no longer assume that all temporary forest clearance is the result of a human attack on the trees.

Radiocarbon dating

In the years following the first definition of the zones, many radiocarbon dates were obtained. Soon, a number of discrepancies became apparent, especially with regard to the correlation of environmental and archaeological data from the later third millennium bc. The basic conflict lies between the pollen evidence for a phase of forest regeneration, Zone C, and the archaeological evidence for a number of late third-millennium structures. These include, from the two areas examined earlier in this chapter, the Walton Heath and Rowland's hurdle trackways, and the Bell tracks and Upper Baker Platform. All told, there are some twenty structures and stray finds which could, on radiocarbon evidence, fit into the phase when forest cover seems to have increased and farming declined. The picture looks busy. On the other hand, because radiocarbon dates are not precise, and represent time spans of a number of decades rather than exact years, both the dating of the structures and that of the Pollen Zones can be argued back and forth over the centuries of the later third millennium bc. Zone C can be interpreted as longer or shorter by a couple of centuries, and almost all the signs of human activity can be argued as dating to the preceding or the following period. The process is a fascinating one if you like puzzles, but infuriating if you want a cut and dried account of prehistory.

fig. 5
fig. 17

It also illustrates well the problems of using radiocarbon dates. The number of dates from the Levels, and the abundance of information about their provenance, has highlighted certain difficulties which simply do not show in contexts where only one or two results are available. For a start, it is still not clear whether a more accurate reflection of past chronologies would be achieved by calibrating the radiocarbon dates, in order to convert them to calendar years. Readers will be aware that radiocarbon years are not the exact equivalent of calendar years, and that 2000 bc (radiocarbon) is about 2500 BC (calendar), whilst 3000 bc is about 3800 BC. So what looks like a millennium is not only further back in time, but also longer than a thousand years. If the Levels' structures dated between 3000 bc and 2000 bc were built over a period of 1300 years, in calendar terms, the degree of activity was slighter than it seems at first sight.

However, there are a number of different calibration curves for radiocarbon dates, from Suess' famous North American bristlecone-pine curve to local floating curves based on Somerset Levels oak, and there are a number of ways of making the necessary calculations. One significant difference is between those charts which present a smooth calibration curve with a steadily increasing divergence between radiocarbon and calendar years back into the past, and those charts which have a number of kinks or wiggles superimposed on the same general trend. The kinks are due to past variation in the amount of carbon-14 in the atmosphere, which has caused radiocarbon dates to be bunched together when the amount decreases and to be absent when it increases. The third millennium bc has a number of wiggles and these could have disturbed the picture of what was happening in the Levels, pulling dates out of a time of increase and bunching them before or after, to give an impression of great activity followed by a lull when really the activity level was steady. Therefore, the decision to calibrate or not, and which calibration curve to use, will affect interpretation of the later Neolithic. We have used a smooth calibration curve, as our diagrams show.

The matter is further complicated by the apparent discrepancy between radiocarbon dates obtained from wood, and those obtained from peat. Samples of peat generally give younger age results than wood, probably due to ground water percolation through the peat. But as peat sequences and peat dates are used for the development of regional and local pollen zones, their correlation with wooden structures dated in isolation is obviously complex. Although we have looked in detail at these problems, we will not pursue them here.

It is the wealth of data available to us from the Levels which underlines the complexity of correlations, and which emphasizes the difficulty of making a chronological interpretation of the Neolithic period. The problems arise in just those areas of interpretation and in the same mid-to-later third millennium bc period which have been a focus of interest for prehistorians of southern Britain in recent years. Some archaeologists studying the Neolithic period have suggested a general mid-millennium forest regeneration accompanied by a decline in archaeological evidence for human activity, and they have done so largely on the correlation of radiocarbon dates from pollen analyses and from archaeological sites, including dates from the Levels. Those readers who have followed the above argument, and perhaps even more so those who have found it confusing, will appreciate that we have doubts about drawing a bold general outline for the period on the basis of such evidence. But one need not be too pessimistic. The challenge is to refine our methods of interpretation, to gain a better understanding of what our data signify, and to explore new ways of understanding the past.

5 Woodland crafts: ancient evidence and modern experiments

... their axes, helved with birch, began to swing in rhythm. At first each hewed a deep notch, chopping steadily at the same spot for some seconds, then the axe rose swiftly and fell obliquely on the trunk a foot higher up; at every stroke a great chip flew, thick as the hand, splitting away with the grain. When the cuts were nearly meeting, one stopped and the other slowed down, leaving his axe in the wood for a moment at every blow; the mere strip, by some miracle still holding the tree erect, yielded at last, the trunk began to lean and the two axemen stepped back a pace and watched it fall. ...

(L. Hémon, 1921)

As our work developed in the Levels, it became apparent that opportunities existed for new investigations into ancient technologies. We were using a variety of environmental approaches, based on plants, pollen, beetles and fungal remains, and the tree-ring work was beginning to expand. It suddenly dawned on us that the scope of our enquiries could be further extended, perhaps endlessly, and the only hindrances were likely to be lack of facilities or reticence in starting new lines of enquiry. As scientists (which archaeologists in wetlands certainly have to be, or pretend to be) we were aware that observations and conclusions based on our unique evidence had to be firmly documented, and preserved for others to see and believe in. All these lines of thought came neatly together through our investigations into prehistoric hurdle tracks of the period c. 2700–1600 bc. Here we were able to refine the tree-ring evidence, to introduce woodland studies in a new way, to begin a series of experiments into wood technology, and to decide on our conservation needs for the future. Although these studies were brought into being through the discovery of the Walton Heath hurdles, we had already excavated one hurdle track. This was a structure found just across from the Eclipse Peat Works; its name, the Eclipse track, was thus not difficult to invent.

Hurdles

Hurdle tracks are not hard to envisage, being merely a series of woven panels (like garden fencing panels) dropped flat onto the marsh and held in place by

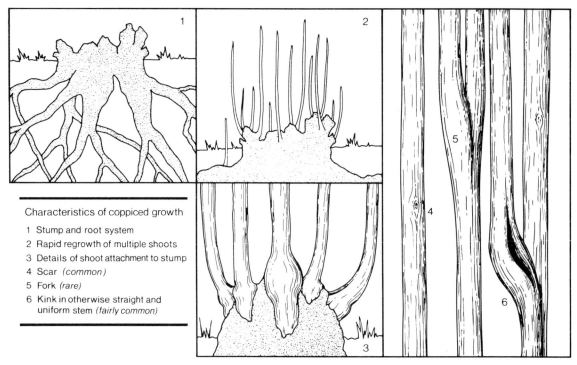

Characteristics of coppiced growth

1 Stump and root system
2 Rapid regrowth of multiple shoots
3 Details of shoot attachment to stump
4 Scar *(common)*
5 Fork *(rare)*
6 Kink in otherwise straight and
  uniform stem *(fairly common)*

25 Diagram to show the identifiable elements in a coppice system.

pegs or poles pushed through them, and forming a wide, relatively flat, flexible walking surface. As we shall see, they make a very effective trackway until the rot sets in. Although we now have evidence of hurdles made at various periods from *c.* 2800 bc right down to the late Iron Age *c.* 200 bc, the Walton Heath and Eclipse hurdles gave us the best evidence for this ancient activity.

Hurdles today are made by experienced craftsmen, and their techniques include some of the features found on the Levels' hurdles. Their raw material comes from managed woodlands where hazel has grown in the light, and where the stools have been kept under control by coppicing. We know from documentary evidence assembled by Oliver Rackham that the medieval techniques of coppicing and pollarding have existed in England for 1000 years, and our evidence now suggests that the record may be extended back at least another 4000 years.

fig. 25 In coppicing, hazel and other woods are cut back every few years, and then encouraged to grow from the stump or stool at a fast rate, to yield crops of straight young rods. The new shoots grow quickly from the stool, and observations show that in one year a hazel rod may stretch upwards (possibly 1 m in the first year) and exceed the growth of an uncoppiced hazel sapling by two to three times. The coppiced shoots are appetizing to cattle, deer or sheep

86

and therefore coppiced areas were traditionally fenced. The shoots may be cut down at regular intervals, e.g. at four, seven or ten years, depending on the length and thickness of the rods needed for fencing, hurdles, plant supports, thatch or other roofing poles, or other uses. The rods are generally taken in an operation called clear-felling, where the whole stool is cleared of all shoots. Some of these will have sprouted more vigorously than others, and will thus be thicker and longer. Felling generally begins after leaf-fall, and further cutting may take place over the winter months until the sap begins to rise again in the spring. The shoots are stored for use, then (if intended for hurdles) split and woven using a wooden break. This is a heavy beam with holes spaced along its length, into which are placed the uprights, called sails; around these are woven the horizontals, called rods, and the rods are often bent around the outside sail and returned into the hurdle. About ten hurdles can be made by an experienced craftsman in a day.

When we first began to study the techniques of prehistoric hurdle-making, we were unable to understand all of the features we uncovered until we had made our own hurdles using comparable hazel sails and rods. Before describing our own efforts, however, it is necessary to look briefly at the genuine articles. The Neolithic hurdles from Walton Heath, and the Bronze Age hurdles of the Eclipse track, were made of hazel rods and sails cut from coppiced woodlands on the Polden Hills or Meare island; hazel would not have grown in the marsh, and no self-respecting hurdle-maker would set up his operations on a soggy, unstable bog. The Walton Heath hurdles were made by a craftsman who used unsplit sails and rods, making an even weave as he passed one rod in front of a sail and behind the next, and reversing the process for the next rod; this is best described as a simple Over and Under weave (with single rods). Some modern hurdles have double or triple rods bunched, to make, for example, a triple Over and triple Under weave. The Walton panels thus made were mostly 2.2–2.5 m long, and 0.7–1.4 m wide, with forty-five to sixty rods and only four to seven sails. Modern panels have more sails set close together, but if unsplit sails and rods are used, the amount of bending of the pieces means that sails have to be more widely spaced. The Walton Heath rods were all the same length in each panel, so that each rod ran the whole length of the panel and its ends stuck out beyond the end-sails. Modern panels have rods twisted and bent back into the panel around an end-sail, and a very firm grip between rods and sails is thus obtained. For the Walton panels, this grip was lacking and they were rather floppy structures, which could be pulled into a parallelogram. In an effort to stop this, the hurdle-maker picked thin willow and hazel shoots which he proceeded to twist and use as rope, tying neat knots and lacing the rope around the ends of sails and rods, to hold them in place; this did not exactly solve the problem of flex, but it helped hold the loose weave until the hurdles were placed in the marsh.

What was striking about the Walton panels was the uniformity of diameter of the rods, with a very large proportion in the range 14–18 mm; this made the

plate 41

plate XI

plate 42

panels smooth and even in appearance, and doubtless easy to weave. Yet when the growth-rings were counted, the age of the rods was seen to be variable, some rods taking nine years to reach a diameter achieved by a neighbour in only three. How can this be so in a coppiced system? The answer seemed clear, that Neolithic man was not clear-felling, but was using a method called draw-felling or drawing, where he only took selected shoots of the required size from the stools, leaving those not needed behind, to grow on for later selection. We can thus envisage a Neolithic woodland as quite unlike a modern coppiced area which is patterned, composed of different areas each with stools at a different stage of growth, a three-year stand or a seven-year stand; instead, our Neolithic woodland was a mosaic of hazel stools of different ages, each likely to yield some shoots of the required size. The system was flexible and successful, to judge by the fine quality of the Walton hurdles, although one problem must have been the actual draw-felling of the stools, as we shall see.

As work progressed in our studies of the Walton Heath structure, a further hurdle track was encountered in the same area. This, Rowland's track, was badly damaged but proved nonetheless to be made of hazel, which is likely to have grown in the same area and at the same time as that from Walton. If so, and the matter is not yet certain, then here was an opportunity to test for tell-tales, that is, the identity of individual craftsmen. No two modern hurdle-makers weave panels in exactly the same way; each has his own technique, and style, in cleaning rods, weaving-in, twisting and bending rods, and finishing-off the panel. In our two Neolithic hurdle tracks, possibly exactly contemporary, we looked for tell-tales. Walton already had several, in the uniformity of rod lengths, in the abundance and character of ties, and in the finishing-off of panels with axework to make straight, even ends and neat sails. Rowland's track proved, to our minds, that a different hurdle-maker had been at work, because he used double or triple sails in some of his panels, he did not use ties at all, and he returned some of the rods into the panel.

We concluded that the Neolithic community on the edge of the Polden Hills had a coppiced woodland and that this was felled at a time when conditions demanded that hurdles be laid in at least two wet places on the raised bog. Two experienced hurdle-makers were then set to work, each responsible for all the hurdles for one particular stretch. The Walton Heath man made at least eighty hurdles, the other man at least twenty.

In 1984 another Neolithic hurdle was discovered, on Meare Heath, and appears to be the earliest yet known from the Levels, and indeed from the whole of Britain. The site, called Franks', had been heavily cut for peat and only part of one hurdle remained. It seems that this was an isolated panel, perhaps floated in from a structure at the edge of the Meare island 200 m to the north. The panel was evenly woven of very slender rods only 7–10 mm in diameter, and it suggests that a well-managed coppice existed c. 2800 bc on Meare island. If so, this is the earliest such woodland system that we know of in Britain, other than that associated with the Sweet Track.

1 Recent floods in the Somerset Levels. Still a common winter event, the water is now largely confined to specific catchments through flood relief schemes.

2 A block of ancient peat, broken apart to show the excellent preservation of macroscopic plant remains. a, twig; b, leaf; c, reed rhizome; d, bogbean.

3 Peat-cutting by hand, early twentieth century. Note the use of spades to cut the blocks or mumps, forks to lift them up and out of the trench, and cider to fuel the operation.

4 Stacking peat to dry, early twentieth century.

5 Brushwood trackway exposed by machine-cutting of the peat. Part of the trackwood has gone through the machine and lies chopped into small pieces in the bottom of the mumps stacked by the machine (behind the scale). The track is dated *c.* 2400 bc.

6 The Abbot's Fishhouse at
Meare, built on the edge of the
medieval Mere-pool.

7 The Abbot's Way, a roadway of *c.* 2000 bc linking the islands of Westhay and Burtle. The
structure was first discovered over 150 years ago. The excavation shown here was one of the
Somerset Levels Project's first major undertakings.

8 The Glastonbury Lake Village excavations of Bulleid and Gray, with a hearth and mound exposed for visitors.

9 Excavation of Mound 13, Glastonbury Lake Village, with radiating floor timbers exposed. In the background is a pump, needed for most of the early excavations due to the then high water-table.

10 (*below*) How the Iron Age settlement of Meare was discovered. Floodwaters cover the low-lying fields, with the mounds of the settlements showing as islands in the sea.

11 (*right*) The Meare Heath track as seen in section by Bulleid in 1933, when he was able to record planks up to 10 m long. The peat-cutters, often paid by yield of peat, found such heavy wooden structures to be hindrances to their work, yet they gave Bulleid and his successors every assistance.

12 Discovery of the Iron Age logboat on Shapwick Heath. Found in *Cladium* peats of the raised bog, this boat provided confirmation of a major episode of flooding in the closing centuries bc.

13 One of the Romano-British hoards found by peat-cutters on Shapwick Heath. The hoards date to the decades around AD 400, and consist of pewter and bronze vessels, and bronze and silver coins.

14 View to the west from the island of Westhay, with targets marking places where the Abbot's Way was identified by small excavations and drilling. The total distance traced in this way was about 1 km.

15 Excavations on the Sweet Track, Drove Site. The diggers' weight is kept off the Neolithic wood by use of modern boxes and planks, and small toe-boards. Markers are used to note the position of wood which is then temporarily protected by a thin covering of wet peat as excavation continues. Polythene bags cover pieces of wood which may project higher.

16 Excavations on the Sweet Track, Drove Site. A general view, with sampling for environmental analyses in middle.

17 The use of toe-boards amidst a welter of Neolithic wood. One of the authors is exposing some pottery fragments with the use of a bamboo spatula.

18 Sealing of a waterlogged site, the Sweet Track,
Turbary Site. Polythene sheeting covers the entire
site, an operation at the end of every day of work
to prevent drying-out of the site overnight. Heavy
rain has temporarily aided the work.

19 The Sweet Track, Railway Site. A portion of
the track, deliberately flooded to highlight the
raised plank walkway. Note the substructure of
rail and crossed pegs, and compare with the
reconstruction shown in plate 20.

20 Experimental reconstruction of the Sweet
Track, with basal rail, crossed pegs and plank
walkway. See also plates 51 and 52.

21 Sweet Track, Railway Site. Here, at the south end of the site, the lines of the Sweet Track (left) and of the slightly lower Post Track (right) can be distinguished.

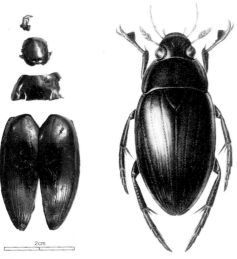

2cm

22 Remains of a water beetle found in association with Sweet Track timbers, and a modern specimen for comparison. The scale is cm.

23 Sweet Track, Turbary Site. A length of track reinforced with triple rails, instead of the normal one rail only, to maintain the height of the walkway across a particularly wet area. The planks which rested upon the rail and peg setting were washed away nonetheless.

24 Sweet Track, Railway Site. Both Sweet and Post Tracks are here, but separated by several metres. The planks of the Post Track (left) were split from lime and ash trunks, whereas those of the Sweet Track (right) were mainly of oak.

26 Sweet Track, Turbary Site. Detail of an oak plank (width 12.5 cm) showing a neatly chopped end and countersunk hole. The plank presumably rested originally on the double rails shown.

25 A peg of hazel from the Sweet Track, Drove Site, showing the well-preserved facets on its lower end. Diameter 80 mm.

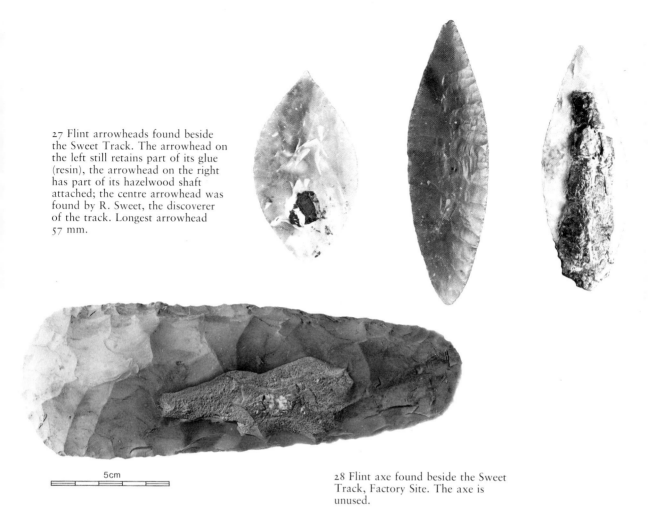

27 Flint arrowheads found beside the Sweet Track. The arrowhead on the left still retains part of its glue (resin), the arrowhead on the right has part of its hazelwood shaft attached; the centre arrowhead was found by R. Sweet, the discoverer of the track. Longest arrowhead 57 mm.

5cm

28 Flint axe found beside the Sweet Track, Factory Site. The axe is unused.

29 Sweet Track, Railway Site. Lying beside an intact part of the track, where the plank is still in place, is an axe blade of jadeite, unused. Its covering board has been removed.

30 Pottery sherds found amidst the wood of the Sweet Track. See fig. 15 for reconstruction drawing.

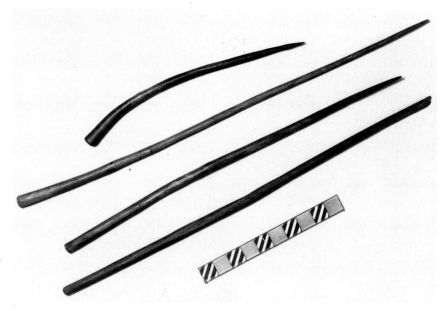

31 Pins of yew wood from the Sweet Track. The scale is 10 cm. The two central pins have slightly straightened during their conservation. The lower piece is an unfinished pin.

32 Wooden dish of oak from the Sweet Track. Length 24 cm.

33 Garvin's brushwood track, *c.* 2400 bc. Coming off the raised bog, two tracks join and continue as a single heavier pathway leading to the Polden Hills (background).

34 The Walton Heath hurdle track, *c.* 2300 bc. Panels woven of coppiced hazel have been laid flat on the surface of a raised bog, and skewered to the surface by long poles pushed through (two may be seen near the scale).

35 The Baker Platform. In use during the second half of the third millennium bc, this platform was the starting point of several routes from the Westhay island.

36 The Bell B track, *c*. 2000 bc, at the Westhay island. A double layer of brushwood and transverses was used to build a thick track leading off the Baker platform. The scale is 6 feet.

50cm

37 An oak digging implement, found amidst the wood of the Baker Platform.

5cm

38 Neolithic mallet of yew, found on Meare Heath. The handle (incomplete) was formed by a side branch, and the mallet head from the trunk of the tree.

39 Wood cut by beaver teeth. The groups of long, narrow, parallel facets are typical of the marks left by beaver incisors. Diameter at base 60 mm.

40 View of flooded land in Canada, caused by beaver damming a small stream. Beaver lodge in the middle of the pond.

41 Detail of a Neolithic hurdle from Walton Heath. The unsplit hazel rods have a single Over-and-Under weave on the hazel sails. Note the uniformity of rod diameters.

42 Withy tie, used to hold together the corner of a hurdle on the Walton Heath track. Many such ties were found.

43 The Eclipse track *c.* 1500 bc. This structure probably required over 1000 hurdles to form a trackway between the island of Meare and the Polden Hills.

Draw-felling in coppiced hazel woodland is an unusual practice today, but it may have been common in the prehistoric Levels. The Eclipse track, a structure consisting of an estimated 1000 hurdles, and dated at least 1000 years later than the Franks' hurdle, and 500 years later than the Walton Heath hurdles, was made of draw-felled hazel, which was used to form panels 2 m long and almost 1 m wide. The supply of long rods was probably restricted, and where a woven rod ended within the panel, another short length was used to complete the weave, but was not thereupon bent back into the panel. The result must have been a very floppy hurdle, which would sag if used upright, and which separated and spread when used flat in the track.

plate 43
plate x

One stretch of the track at the southern end (East Moors) was in a fairly decayed state when it was used by someone whose feet crashed through the thin rods, leaving imprints behind which were then covered by replacement panels put on the damaged portions. When we came to examine this track, we could identify rods side-by-side with diameters of 17–18 mm, yet their ages ranged from four to nine years; they were certainly draw-felled, and in the more normal winter months, judging by their outermost growth-ring. To make over 1000 hurdles for a trackway, using up 80,000 m of hazel rods of uniform diameters, plus sails, must have drained supplies and exhausted the woodland for a few years.

Experiments in hurdle-making

The excavations along both the Eclipse and the Walton Heath tracks attracted the interest of modern hurdle-makers, and as a result of their enquiries and comments we decided to conduct a time-trial in hurdle-making. In a preliminary note about the Walton panels, we had suggested that a large heavy hurdle might take ten hours to make; this led Richard Darrah of the West Stow Anglo-Saxon Village, among others, to suggest we had grossly overestimated the hours and underestimated the hurdle-makers of the past. He was right, as our combined experiments showed.

We were offered coppiced hazel in Bradfield Woods, Suffolk, by the Society for the Promotion of Nature Reserves, and in 1976 a team of three attacked several stools which carried three- and five-year shoots. Neolithic stone axes were used, hafted in ash, together with hand-held flint flakes, and a modern billhook of iron. We wanted to draw-fell shoots of 15–25 mm diameter, but to do so we had to clear other unwanted shoots as well, in order to get at the desired shoots with the axe; draw-felling was obviously not as selective and exclusive as we had thought. The best way to obtain the shoots was to bend them down from the stool onto the ground, and then stamp on them and try to break them off. With a subsequent twist and pull, this often worked, and the axe could also be directed into the weak junction of shoot and stool. Dry shoots, in late summer, could be broken more easily than the sappy, wet, flexible shoots of springtime.

plate 44   We found that the stone axes had to be directed very accurately, or else they bounced off the wood, and, early on in the proceedings, a timed experiment had to be abandoned as an axe flew from the haft and skidded over the ground and into a mole hole, and many precious minutes were lost before its recovery. Perhaps this may explain the large number of stray Neolithic axes? The binding of the axe to the haft is crucial. Various stools with usable shoots were cleared by axe, hand or foot. The shoots were then cleaned and twigs and leaves removed using flint flakes, although hand-stripping alone was often as effective.

plate 46   Six sturdy sails were then selected, stuck into the ground, and the weaving of rods began. With a simple Over and Under weave, the panel grew until at rod fifteen it began to twist, because at each end of the panel the thick rod-ends had been woven uniformly, and stuck out on one side only. We then put a double weave in, but reversed the second rod so that its thin end was on top of the previous rod's thick end, and continued the new regime. This at once corrected the twist; later we examined our records for Walton Heath and noted the existence of double rods precisely at points where a twist might have been apparent. We had to let in doubles at three levels of the experimental panel, and it is likely that the Walton Heath hurdle-makers would also have done this, but their rods were much more uniform overall than ours, so this problem was probably not as great. The weave completed, the panel was trimmed at the ends, a few ties were attempted to secure sail and rod junctions, and the panel was then uprooted and carried from the woods on the head of one man; it weighed 30 kg. The whole operation took us one and a half hours, and three men were one too many: too many cooks, too many weavers. Two persons were ideal, and they could complete the task in one and a half to two hours. The experiment demonstrated the effectiveness of stone axes, the difficulty of draw-felling and ease of weaving with the occasional double rod, and the strength and flexibility of the panel: it highlighted for us all the skills of the hurdle-makers of the Neolithic.

Conservation

Because we had already realized that the Walton Heath hurdles were unique in the woodland information they held, we decided in 1975 not only to excavate and record, but also to try and conserve one complete hurdle. We had our Project laboratory, of which more will be said later, but no tank large enough to take a hurdle measuring almost 3 m long and over 1 m wide and constructed of some seventy pieces of thin hazel rods and sails, and several ties of hazel and willow, all severely degraded and resting on wet peat. Our first problem was how to get it out of the bog.

With a small team of volunteers, we isolated the hurdle by removing all other hurdles and stray pieces of wood. It was then undercut, and pieces of

plate 47   marine plywood passed beneath to make a platform upon which the hurdle rested, with 5–10 cm of peat between ply and panel. Steel rods were bolted to the plywood to make a firm base, and the next stage was to lift the whole thing, carry it over a ditch and put it on a lorry's flatbed; our team of eight was inadequate for the task, as the structure weighed over half a tonne, it was December, cold and wet, and we had been working all day at the platform-making. A handy tractor and chain soon hauled the structure out, and we then lifted it onto the lorry. Thereafter the task was supposed to be easier. A contract had been agreed with the National Museum of Antiquities of Scotland to conserve the hurdle by acetone-rosin; this involves acetone baths to dissolve resins, and impregnation with rosin in acetone, thus creating rosin crystals within the wood structure. The hurdle was taken by us to Edinburgh, put into a new, huge stainless steel tank, and thence lifted over rooftops into the laboratory, where it rested until the fire authorities, and conservators, decided that acetone – which is volatile and flammable – was not a good idea here. The hurdle was lifted out over the rooftops again and taken to a new laboratory, which was found to be near a gas-works, and so it rested again. After almost two years, a new conservator, Tom Bryce, arrived in Edinburgh and he decided to abandon the acetone-rosin process and conserve the hurdle on its peat bed by polyethylene glycol (PEG), the process we had been using with some success in the Levels (see below).

The panel was soaked in a weak solution of PEG, then drained and impregnated by spraying and painting with PEG for many months, with a humidity cover over the tank. Finally, the hurdle was considered to be stable enough, and its peat base secure, for transport back to the Levels, and to its final resting place in the County Museum Taunton; after a crane-lift off the lorry, it had its last laugh on the way into the museum by getting stuck on the cobbled path, jamming in doorways, and smashing several fingers. It is now on display along with other material from the Levels, and it has been seen by many people. But to maintain it for the future, it requires stable conditions of 45–60 per cent relative humidity and a temperature of 10–15°C, neither of which it receives consistently. RIP.

plate 48

We have already mentioned the need to conserve some of our evidence for future studies. Although discoveries had been made in the peat for many years, only a few objects had ever been conserved, and the rest were thrown away or left to disintegrate. It is easy to observe the stages in such destruction of a wet piece of prehistoric wood, a peg for example, from drying of the surface, surface cracks, twisting and warping, major cracks, to splitting open, so that what began as a complete, round stem will end as a wedge, like a third of a pie or cake. Conservators regularly disbelieve the amount of shrinkage that is possible until it occurs on their desks over a matter of weeks. The reason the wooden objects from the Levels act like this is that they are so degraded; they have undergone deterioration by hydrolysis, or chemical decomposition. The cell walls have disintegrated, leaving the wood visually intact but very soft and heavily waterlogged, and sometimes the object will have the consistency of

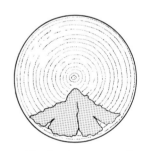

26 Sketch of a section of roundwood from the prehistoric peats, with its final stage of shrinkage after exposure and entirely natural drying.

plates XII, XIII

cream cheese. However, if we were excavating a site full of prehistoric pottery, or flints, we would not throw all except the prettiest pieces away, even if many were plain, ordinary, rather boring fragments. The excavation of wooden objects, many of which are also plain and ordinary, should be no different; we have an obligation to save as many as possible, to fulfil the requirements of future archaeology. Wetlands will not last for ever, and we may well be the last to see prehistoric wooden artifacts still in the peat.

The conservation process most commonly used for waterlogged wood is impregnation by polyethylene glycol (PEG 4000), used as we have seen for preserving one of the hurdles. We have tried other methods, freeze-drying among them, but none is as successful for our wood as PEG. PEG is a non-hygroscopic wax which will give strength to degraded wood. The material, in various grades (we use the heavy grade), has been used for many years and is generally good at preventing distortion and cracking. The excavated wood which comes to the laboratory is recorded by photography, bandaged completely, and tied gently on metal grids; several layers of wood can thus be lowered into fibreglass tanks and held at different heights, with the heaviest wood at the bottom. Heating panels in the tank base are controlled by thermostats. The initial solution is a cold soak of $\frac{1}{4}$ PEG and $\frac{3}{4}$ water, and after an interval the heaters are switched on. Over a period of six months, the thermostats are turned up and up, until 50°C is reached; by this time much of the water has been evaporated from the solution, and drawn out of the wood, and the level of liquid maintained by adding melted PEG. After about nine months in all, the solution is as much as 90 per cent PEG, and the wood is removed, unbandaged and wiped clean; the wax hardens and soon the artifact is firm and able to be handled freely, when it is recorded again for any changes that may have taken place.

The bare outline given above of the process we use conceals the very great problems we encountered in the early days of our conservation work, with leaking tanks, popping heaters, failed thermostats, power cuts, and the need to continually boil up wax using primitive burners and containers. Our field assistants never suspected that this would be one of their major tasks when appointed to the job, but all coped remarkably well, and some even became expert electricians, and plumbers, by the end. Among more serious problems encountered by the Project was the fact that our lab was originally placed on the peat near a small railway line which carried peat-wagons to the factory. The vibration from the wagons shook the ground over a wide area, and the entire laboratory would tremble as trains passed, and our electrical junctions jumped about with disastrous results. We eventually moved the whole laboratory to firmer ground. The occasional power failures were overcome by installing a generator which could provide the power to run the heaters at crucial times. A tank full of high-concentration melted PEG, and no heating, will soon turn into a solid block of wax, thus destroying wood, heaters and probably tank.

We cannot close this account of techniques without referring to our first efforts at conservation. In 1975 we had no laboratory, office or storerooms, yet we had begun to accumulate Bronze Age and Neolithic wooden artifacts in tubs and in wooden boxes lined with plastic sheets. We rented a small house and turned its one bedroom into a conservation lab. We put wood and fishtank heaters and thermometers into tanks of wood lined with thick polythene sheets, and began the process. The obvious things began to happen. The wallpaper peeled, the electrics began to fuse with the damp, and, worse, the tanks began to leak wax solution onto the floor. As soon as we could, we brought in plastic tanks and began to transfer the wood and wax from old to new tanks; the operation was incredibly messy, and the floor was like a skating rink. In mid-flow there was a knock on the door – it was the landlord with his daughter who had just arrived from America for a visit, and wanted to meet the new tenants! We shouted, 'watch out, the floor is slippery', but too late and a body skidded across the room. Soon afterwards, by mutual agreement, we moved from the house into a new portable lab.

We should not forget that what has been conserved is a small proportion of what there was. To have conserved several thousand prehistoric wooden artifacts is, we think, a unique achievement in Britain, but in doing so we have had to discard (after recording) thousands of others.

After conservation, the wood can be handled more freely than before, and woodworking details examined and felt in ways which would be likely to damage the exceedingly soft ridges and facets, and edges, of prehistoric artifacts. This has allowed us to think more carefully about woodmanship, about the felling, splitting and trimming of pieces before they were incorporated in the tracks and platforms and subsequently submerged by peat. One obvious example of this is the beaver-chewed wood from the Baker Platform (chapter 4), which was identified as such only upon reflection during and after conservation of the pieces, and after we had unsuccessfully tried to duplicate the facets with stone axe and flint knife.

Experiments in woodworking

Experimenting with wood has always been one of the ways by which we have hoped to gain a better understanding of ancient techniques. Whether it is just working with a single piece of wood, or actually building a track, new thoughts always arise, and we now know more about prehistoric skills by trying to acquire them. One of our experiments was concerned with felling trees in order to test various axes. We borrowed Neolithic and Bronze Age axes of stone and bronze from a museum, were permitted to sharpen their blades, and hafted them with ash handles. In sharpening, we sometimes left a   plate 49 nick or irregularity in the blade, and found that after hard use these were generally eliminated; the implications of this for our further work are discussed in the next chapter.

Felling of alder, hazel and birch trees was easy with most of the axes, although stone axes tended to bounce off the fibrous birchwood in particular, rather than making a clean cut. The stone axes were much thicker than the bronze axes, and it was necessary to chop a wide notch into the trees as otherwise the blade jammed.

plate 45
Bronze axes, particularly flat axes, were more efficient in felling these trees because of the thin blades and a slightly sharper cutting edge. For oak and ash trees, our work also showed that stone axes were very efficient if the axemen themselves were efficient and in good condition; it was imperative to chop accurately to avoid bouncing the axes off the cut notches. The chips detached by stone axes from all of the trees were short and rather smashed, unlike the long, cleaner chips produced by metal axes. We also tried to chop through seasoned oak and ash, and found this to be very difficult with stone axes. All of these initial experiments could only make us appreciate more readily the skills of Early Neolithic man who, armed with stone axes, could and did fell massive oaks 400 years old and fully 1 m across, as well as thousands of hazel, alder, and other trees, simply to create a pathway across the swamp. We also learned not to use the axes as levers, in bending the tree, or in pulling a jammed blade from a notch; it is the easiest way to split an expensive ash handle.

The planks of the Neolithic and Bronze Age structures were our next investigation, and here we relied again upon the skill of Richard Darrah in learning how to split oak and ash trees into halves, then quarters, and into thin planks which were formed by wedging down the converging rays, to make radially split planks. Only seasoned oak wedges and wooden mallets were needed for this, and in one experiment Darrah produced a thin oak plank 3 m long from a massive halved oak in only ninety seconds! The wedges often made burr marks down the plank faces, and splinters of oak might remain in places where the split was not clean. Having seen this, we looked at the conserved planks from the Sweet Track and found plenty of such traces still remaining and not clearly identified during excavation. Splitting of ash was more difficult, but could be done by careful positioning of wedges. Of the other woods, birch was very difficult and this may well account for the total absence of any split birch planks from the Levels. Seasoned oak, and alder too, would pose problems, and this suggests that oak trees felled and then split into planks in the Neolithic and Bronze Age were green and not dry.

An instructive aspect of woodworking preserved in the peats is the sharpening of posts, pegs and stakes for driving into the swamp, marsh or moor. From the Sweet Track there are thousands of heavy pegs prepared in various ways, and bearing clear axe-facets. Almost all the structures have such traces, either on pegs or on the brushwood ends, and there is much information to be gained from their study. Our experiments on hazel, ash,
plate 50
willow, alder, birch and oak were aimed at this, and we chopped through hundreds of pieces of roundwood at various angles and with various axes, in order to record the problems and the facets. The clear facets left in hazel, ash

and alder by all tools were matched by comparable facets on prehistoric wood, but our efforts on willow with a stone axe left only blurred facets due to crushing of the wood; yet the willow from the Sweet Track has very clean and clear facets, produced we think by a very sharp, thin stone or flint axe, or possibly a jadeite one. Blurred facets on birch were, however, exactly matched on the prehistoric wood from many structures on Walton Heath and the Westhay Level.

The facets left by the axes in our experiments were very closely comparable to those found on prehistoric roundwood, and help us identify types of blade, and techniques, in ancient woodworking. Stone axes tend to leave slightly dished facets if the latter are viewed across their width, but so do socketed bronze axes; the facets however are often different in length, the sharpness of the intersections between them differs, and the angle at which the blade entered and left the wood varies according to whether it was stone or metal. Axemen of the Neolithic knew their tools well, and knew that their blades were rarely sharp enough, and that most were too fat (the axes not the men) to try to make very long, shallow-angled facets on a piece of roundwood. Instead they would chop at a steeper angle, to form a sharp but thick point, then and only then attempt to thin the stem by an upper, more shallow chop-mark, taking off the first intersection of facet and bark. We could reproduce this sequence easily.

Bronze Age axemen, however, with thinner, sharper blades, could try (often without success) to do the job in one, with a very fierce chop at a shallow angle well up from the intended point. If it worked, the piece had a long, flat facet but if it did not work, the axe blade stopped within the wood, and was roughly yanked out leaving behind a cut-mark of the exact curvature of the blade; a further, less ambitious blow then produced a point of sorts. Again we could reproduce this sequence, which was both optimistic and realistic. Our use of bronze axes with damaged or rough blades suggested that we might be able to identify individual axes through the ridges left on the facets, and this we have done for a Bronze Age complex.

For oak, we had other experiments to perform, among them the cutting of mortise holes in planks, and the preparation of long, thin stakes from split oak adzed or axed into shape. Holes were made with stone axes by chopping across the grain on both faces at either end, then splitting along the grain between the two cuts to detach the chunk of wood and leave a hole; such holes were thus not truly countersunk, and definitions in future have to be more precise. With bronze axes, all this work could be done from one face only. Stakes could be neatly axed into shape, leaving dozens of dished facets just like those so beautifully preserved on Bronze Age stakes. Work with a palstave mounted as an adze – the blade thus mounted at right angles to a normal axe-mounting – was instructive, and as long as we did not allow the blade to swing gently into our toes, it produced a very smooth surface on oak, leaving no facets at all. We think, in fact, that any adzeman of quality would leave no sign of his blade on ancient wood, and that facets often described as adze-marks are axed, not adzed.

The Sweet Track rebuilt

Experiments have been one of the ways by which we try to better our understanding of the prehistoric structures we excavate, and when these can be combined with public displays there is much to be said for the approach.

plate 20 Recently we were asked to build a stretch of the Sweet Track for a film, and in doing this we were able to try out various ideas about the track and its components.

We obtained an oak tree from a nature reserve in Suffolk, split into heavy but suitable planks by Darrah, and we felled alder, willow and hazel trees to make rails and pegs. As it was the fitting together that was being investigated, we did not hesitate to use modern axes for the felling, although we might well have been accused of 'shortcutting'. Having located a wet, marshy area (the remnants of an old peat-cut) the experiment began. The hardest work was dragging or carrying heavy rails and planks onto the track site; these weighed 50–70 kg each, and the ground was soft and wet, with tall sweetgrass, reed mace and other aquatic plants, and an abundance of buzzing fauna too. The

plates 51 52 rails were hauled into place, and pegs mallet-driven in criss-cross fashion over them. Various sets of pegs were driven, to form V-shapes above the rails, and it became clear at once that the pegs had to be evenly sized and driven at equal angles if the plank was to sit over the rail and lie flat and horizontal. Extra pegs driven in beneath previous pegs helped to correct any sagging on one side, and if the whole plank was too low compared to the one before it, then an extra rail could be placed on top of the first one and pegged in, and this raised the plank substantially. If the plank in question was too high, it was because the peg angles were too steep, or the rail too thin, and to correct this it was necessary to smash the peg top downwards to decrease the angle from the horizontal; this resulted in squashed peg tops and broken pegs if too forceful a blow was delivered.

All these features were noted during our many excavations of the Sweet Track: even-sized pegs in pairs, equal angles of driving, extra pegs, extra rails, bent peg tops, broken pegs, and their functions and positions were clearly fundamental to the long line of horizontal and even planks held firmly between pairs of pegs. The weight of timber and roundwood in the Sweet Track was estimated at 200 tonnes as a result of this experiment, and the major tasks confronting the builders were the felling, possibly the splitting, and certainly the transport of all this wood into and through the swamp. We think it likely that the first planks were put into position as soon as one or two rails were pegged down; it was much easier to drag or carry in the next rails and planks along the plank walk rather than through the soggy marsh. Once on site, therefore, the construction was simple and swift, and on the basis of our admittedly short experiment (10 m of track built) we think that only a hundred man-hours of work could do the job of fitting together all the components to make a track almost 2 km long. This could mean ten men doing the whole thing in a (long) day! But many days were spent assembling the materials, do not forget. This experiment in no way reduced our admiration of the Sweet Track; the structure was clearly so well-researched, designed and engineered that it must rank as one of the best pieces of pre-fabrication in the Neolithic of Britain.

6 Tracks into the high bog: Bronze Age patterns

> The valley was so choked with fog that one could scarcely
> see a cow's length across a field. Every blade, twig, bracken-
> frond, and hoof-print carried water, and the air was filled
> with the noise of rushing ditches. . . .
>
> (R. Kipling 1914)

By the end of the third millennium, the Levels consisted of a vast expanse of
bogland stretching from the Polden Hills northwards to the outskirts of the
Mendips, with only the major islands of rock or sand providing stable and dry
ground. The wetlands had developed into raised bog, with a few patches of
fenwood fringing the bleak expanse, and to the north-east a 'gloomy waste of
waters, or still more hideous expanse of reeds and other aquatic plants,
impassable by human foot, and involved in an atmosphere pregnant with
pestilence and death', as a much later account rather colourfully described
them. Raised bogs depend entirely upon rainfall for their existence, and they
develop an extremely acidic regime where only particular plants such as
Sphagnum moss, cotton-grass and heather may survive and thrive. The surface
of a raised bog is like a gently domed cushion, and the German word
Hochmoor and Swedish *Högmosse* are aptly descriptive. At the edges of the
raised bog, where it is physically contained by island or hillside, there may be a
rand or rather steep slope downwards, to a peripheral channel or lagg, where
surface waters collect from both bog and highland. The waters here are not
fully acidic as part of their source is in the base-rich rocks, of the Poldens in the
south, the islands in the centre, and the Mendip outcrops in the north. As a
result, the dominant plant of the raised bog, *Sphagnum*, cannot colonize the
lagg and the spread of the raised bog is controlled.

Sphagnum moss is an extraordinarily diverse and fascinating species.
Individually small, the mosses form colonies, each dependent upon its own
particular habitat. The common, bright-green mats of *S. cuspidatum* lie
submerged or nearly so in bog pools, while the builders of the bog hummocks,
preferring more aerated conditions, form bright-crimson clumps in which *S.
rubellum* and *magellanicum* dominate. There are many other varieties as well,
and most possess the virtue (for them) of retaining water through quite
extraordinary physical characteristics, in both root system and leaf capacities.
Moss is well-known as a garden aid, conserving water and minerals in dry
soils, and providing a weed-free base for seedlings. It was used in the 1914–18

War as field dressing, to absorb blood and poisonous substances from wounds, and it serves as an effective nappy in other circumstances.

Another conspicuous plant was *Eriophorum*, cotton-grass, or horse's tail, which invades the shallow water of raised bog pools and by mid-summer produces displays of silky, silvery-white tufts which may survive for several months. Stem-bases of cotton-grass clutter up the raised bog peats and are universally detested by peat-diggers and archaeologists for their flexible, dense mats which defy spades and spatulas alike. These and other plants formed the raised bogs, within which dark, acidic pools of open water were prominent, with slow trickles of water easing through cracks and around plant tussocks towards the rand or edge of the bog. Brilliantly coloured at times, dark and dismal at others, the bogs dominated the Brue valley.

plate IV

It was within and upon such an unpromising landscape that the events of the second and earlier first millennium took place. This period, generally described as the Bronze Age, very dramatically divides into two episodes of human activity in the Levels, the first of containment followed by one of expansion. Before examining these, however, let us reflect on the development of the archaeology of this period as it has in effect both directed and restricted our knowledge.

Raised bog peats form through the annual dying and waterlogging of plants, and anything that happens to be laid upon a surface one year will in due time become incorporated in the upward growth of the bog. Over many hundreds of years, a boat may be incorporated in peats, which themselves eventually come to lie beneath a wooden track, itself submerged by further peat formation. It is the same effect as a stratified urban deposit, with Roman remains below medieval below Victorian, but in peat the deposits burying the remains develop from beneath. And of course a flat object like a boat or track bundle may be rafted upwards before coming to a stationary position. And a heavy object may sink into the bog before it too becomes stable. The implications for archaeological stratigraphies are self-evident.

Even with these problems, it is obvious that the latest objects which were somehow put into the bog will have come to rest in the uppermost levels, and will be the first to go if the peat is cut or otherwise removed. As we have seen in chapters 1 and 2, cutting around the villages of Edington and Catcott Burtle, and probably those of Meare, Shapwick and Westhay as well, has been underway for many centuries and so we have lost peat deposits that doubtless contained finds relevant to our prehistoric story. In the absence of major pumping operations to drain the peat, cutting was restricted to the upper peats which were not as wet and waterlogged as lower deposits, and therefore the discoveries made were mostly of the Iron Age and the later Bronze Age, that is, of the first millennium bc. As we have seen, cutting had also taken place in the Westhay Level where the removal of lower peats had exposed the Abbot's Way, and where Godwin could be shown parts of the great complex of Neolithic tracks. The later peats had long been removed from this area, and

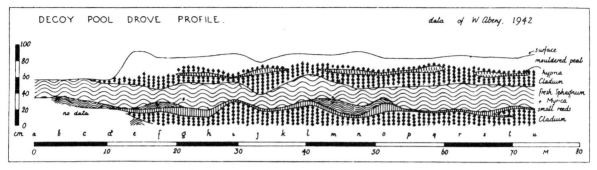

27 *Section of peat at Decoy Pool Drove on Shapwick Heath, drawn by Godwin, with raised bog peat and flooding horizons of Cladium peat. This section is one of the strongest pieces of evidence for the existence of major flooding horizons in the first millennium bc.*

with them a likely yield of archaeological evidence matching that on Shapwick and Meare Heaths, but which was never recorded. The probable loss of archaeological evidence in early peat-cutting is epitomized in the massive extraction ordered by the Abbot of Glastonbury, noted in chapter 1. On Shapwick Heath, Godwin began his great campaign on the upper, as yet uncut peats, and he was able to record in 1937 the basic stratigraphical succession which we have consistently found throughout the northern Levels (chapter 2). By 1942, he was searching for the uppermost peats, and feared that cutting had destroyed the final stages of bog formation. In that year, a section on Decoy Pool Drove gave him the record he wanted, and furthermore allowed him to establish the model of flooding horizons which has dominated studies of the

fig. 27   later peats ever since. The observable peats on Decoy Pool Drove consisted of a deposit of raised bog peat overlain by a *Cladium* peat. *Cladium mariscus* is giant sword sedge, and grows in wet fens which have a moderate to high base status, not at all that of an acidic raised bog. It therefore signifies that flooding-in of waters from the surrounding hills and slopes must have occurred. Above the sedge peats, a layer of reeds marked a shallowing of the fen, and then typical raised bog peats appeared again with the usual mosses and cotton-grass. Moreover, within this upper raised bog peat was a second, thinner layer of *Cladium* peat, marking a second flooding episode in this part of the Levels. These were important observations for Godwin and his collaborators, because when they turned to the archaeological evidence already at hand, they believed they could relate the structures to the flooding horizons. It seemed obvious that if a passage across the drier parts of a raised bog had been established, and it became wet and then wetter, some efforts might be made to maintain the route by building a trackway. When conditions got too bad, and major flooding occurred, the trackways would have to be abandoned and people would swim (unlikely), take to raft or boat, or find another land route.

Our own work in the past decade has helped to define the nature of the flooding while at the same time posing problems over the universality of particular episodes. Girling's study of the remains of beetles on Meare Heath is perhaps the most elegant, if beetles can be elegant. From a monolith taken through some 150 cm of peat, she was able to recognize two horizons of flooding. The first was marked dramatically by the almost total replacement of insects of raised bog character by those of fen type, thus suggesting that the raised bog here had been completely inundated by calcareous waters from the hillslopes, islands and upstream basins of water-courses. The bog surface immediately prior to this major flooding was wetter than before, suggesting that conditions were deteriorating steadily when some event occurred which caused a massive influx of water from the hills. This event has several possible causes, which are discussed below, and need not be entirely or at all climatically induced; its common definition as the Sub-Boreal/Sub-Atlantic climatic transition, with almost universal implications, is only one possibility and one that looks increasingly unlikely as the sole cause of flooding.

The Meare Heath track

In 1941, Godwin and A. R. Clapham attempted to rediscover the Meare Heath track. This very substantial structure had been first noted in peat-cuts by Bulleid in 1890 when he was searching for mounded lake villages. In 1933, he found time to examine part of the track where it had again been chopped through by peat-cutters. The peat had been about 2 m thick over the track but by 1933 only about 50 cm remained. As the track ran roughly north–south (between the Meare village and the Polden Hills), Bulleid could follow its *fig. 28* course along the peat-cuts which were also aligned in the same direction and which therefore had sliced through the track length in various of the short cuttings. One of the pieces of wood noted by Bulleid was a plank of oak 4–7 *plate 11* inches (10–15 cm) thick and 34 feet (10 m) long.

By 1941, the Meare Heath track had been destroyed in many parts of its full length of 2 km or more, but Godwin found it in the side of a peat bank which carried the railway wagons full of peat blocks to the Eclipse Peat Works. At once, he says, he could see that the track lay on the upper surface of raised bog peats, with 10 cm of dark, humified heather peat over the wood; above this was 8 cm of bog myrtle peat, perhaps representing a transitional zone to the *Cladium* sedge fen peat which thereupon succeeded it. This fen peat was clearly Godwin's major flooding horizon and he interpreted the track as a response to worsening conditions which finally overwhelmed the structure completely. A radiocarbon date of *c.* 900 bc from one of the track pegs, allied to clear mortising and sharpening of timber planks and stakes, indicated to him that the track was of the later Bronze Age.

Bulleid, and Godwin after him, described the Meare Heath track as built of oak planks laid transversely to the line, pegged into place by long stakes driven through holes in the planks, with a substructure of birch and alder brushwood, and long squared 'stringers' laid along the sides of the track. These stringers

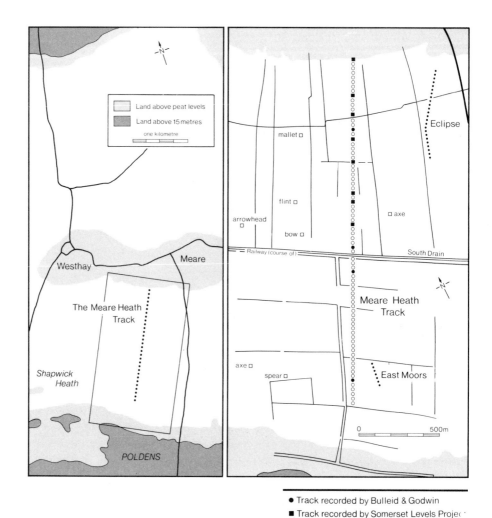

● Track recorded by Bulleid & Godwin
■ Track recorded by Somerset Levels Project

28 Map of Meare Heath with various Bronze Age trackways and other finds shown.

were like bumpers, to keep putative wheeled vehicles on the track. The reconstruction was based entirely upon the longitudinal sections of the track exposed by peat-cutters; after 1941 the area was generally abandoned and allowed to regenerate woodland which masked the old heads. In 1973, major felling took place on Meare Heath and it became clear that the time, almost the last time, to observe and record the trackway had come. An old drove-road plate 53 running east–west across Meare Heath still retained an extra 1 m of peat, and here it was that the track was found and excavated by the Project. It proved to be a rewarding experience, with the upper part of the structure removed in summer heat and the lower part under snow in spring 1975. Contrary to expectations, the track was not basically a transverse structure (like the

Abbot's Way) but consisted of paired, wide planks running longitudinally plates 54, 55 upon transverse bearers held by stakes. The stringers observed by Bulleid were only the sides of the long planks, their bodies having either rotted away, or been removed through peat-cutting along the line. Our clear observation at once removed the possibility of wheeled vehicles, as nowhere would a track *fig. 29* surface exist that was wide enough or junction-smooth. There is no reason, however, to doubt any of Bulleid's observations of this or other structures; he recorded what he saw, and drew an interpretation based on that, and had we excavated at any other less well-protected place along the Meare Heath track we could not have doubted his work, as conditions on our other sites were generally very poor and little remained of any of the upper planks.

Of these other sites, we need only mention one, the northernmost site. By 1977, we had examined several rather sorry parts of the track and begun to assess the evidence that suggested the structure was effectively dead and gone, cut away or lost by drying-out, over most of the 2000 m of its former course. Our field archaeologists, Stephen Coleman and Veryan Heal, had sighted the track line to within the final pasture field before the gentle slope up to Meare island began. They crossed from the dark peat-cuts to the field and searched an abandoned overgrown ditch, which seemingly cut through the track line. To their astonishment, a hefty plank was clearly visible, sticking out from the peat into the ditch; it was a track plank, surviving here *in situ* even if dried-out and plate 56 very hard, and its underside still had the clear facets of Bronze Age axework. Where else could such evidence survive except in wet peats, regularly flooded by ditches cleared only occasionally, when obstructions were left rather than ripped out? It will be clear that much of the Meare Heath track has now gone, through peat-cutting, desiccation or excavation. But to our surprise, an

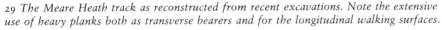

29 *The Meare Heath track as reconstructed from recent excavations. Note the extensive use of heavy planks both as transverse bearers and for the longitudinal walking surfaces.*

undamaged length, more or less in the middle of the peat-cutting area, was discovered in 1984; its preservation is discussed in chapter 8.

Of the track itself only a few more observations need be made. Built of oak planks, both transverse and longitudinals, it was early argued that some of these had come from older dismantled structures, and the prospect of re-assembling a Bronze Age shed or wagon was exciting. But, alas, the tree-ring studies by Morgan soon put paid to this hope; all the wood was felled at about the same time and the rings show that only rather small trees of 100–150 years' age, 30–50 cm across, were taken. Probably this means that only secondary oak woodlands were growing on the Poldens and Meare island, as the use of bronze axe and wooden wedge could certainly cope with a tree of any size, as did stone axe and wedge for the Sweet Track some 2000 years earlier. Many of the Meare Heath timbers were split and axed tangentially, across the rays (a much more difficult task than splitting along the rays), thus achieving a wider plank; this suggests that the woodmen wanted wide planks but, like their predecessors at the south end of the Sweet Track, they did not have the trees. We think that about 180 oaks were needed to build the whole track.

plate 57   The axework on the planks and stakes of the track was well preserved on the first site we excavated, and clearly dished facets were evident. The holes in the transverse planks were neatly cut squares, which we know can be achieved by a sharp bronze axe and wedge, and each of the longer transverses had two such neat holes for the stakes and a third more roughly cut hole at one end. As these superfluous holes were not all on the same side of the track, they did not hold posts for a railing or rope; we think they were used in hauling down the planks from the oak woodlands on the hills and island after felling and splitting. A mere notch at the end would have also allowed the rope to pinch-in and hold the heavy timber, but if any water had to be crossed, such as a lagg, then a rope tied through a hole would be safer.

The Meare Heath trackway runs right across the bog, and so we might infer the existence of two areas of interest to the inhabitants of the Levels who built it: an area on Meare island with pasture and arable fields as well as woodlands, and a likely equivalent on the Polden Hills to the south. Between the two, the track was built when it became evident that the intervening bog was beginning to get increasingly wet.

The evidence for this scenario comes not only from the archaeological excavations and beetle analysis but also from the careful pollen analytical work of Beckett who has refined the pioneer work of Godwin. In chapter 4, the local Pollen Zones A, B and C were noted, in which the first clearances by man were associated with Zone B, succeeding and preceding zones of forest cover where elm, oak and lime dominated, with hazel and other trees and shrubs also present in abundance. The succeeding Zones D and E show little fundamental variation from C except in a slight elm decline in D, and reassertion in E; it is possible that Zone D represents minor forest clearances taking place during the first part of the second millennium bc, but by c. 1400 bc the forests had regenerated. We have relatively little archaeological evidence for the period 1900–1200 bc either in tracks or artifacts with the exceptions of the Eclipse hurdle track noted in chapter 5 and a few finds noted below. Then, in the closing centuries of the millennium, the pollen indicates that a major clearance of woodland took place, and it is during this Zone F that the Meare Heath track, and many others, were built. The clearance phase lasted until *c.* 500 bc, with a possible slight regeneration of woodland after this, followed by more widespread and long-lasting clearances (see chapter 7).

The first major clearance, Zone F, involved the felling of trees such as elm and lime, opening up of the drier land for pasture and arable cultivation, and maintenance of some oak woodlands (which provided track timbers) with hazel as under-storey or as separate coppice stands. Within this episode, there occurred the first major flooding of the bogland, so well-marked by beetle studies and tied in to the pollen sequence by joint sampling and collaborative studies carried out by Girling and Beckett. The invasion of giant sedges and establishment of a fen over the lower parts of the raised bog permitted water beetles, waterside beetles and mud beetles to flourish, and dung beetles found near the Meare Heath track suggest the presence of grazing animals nearby on Meare island. Pollen of plantain and other plants suggests grassland, and weeds of disturbed ground indicate arable fields on Meare island as well. The track itself gives the most tangible evidence of the interest which local communities took in the Levels at this time, but these other lines of enquiry provide the reasons why such a structure was needed.

A few other archaeological finds on Meare Heath, including dumps of wood and other slighter trackways near the Polden slope, complement the picture; bronze axes, spearheads, and a flint sickle blade suggest activities concerned with the woodland, the hunt, and the harvest. Of settlement itself, we know little, but a wider assessment is given later in this chapter.

plate 58

The Shapwick Heath complex

In 1947, another heavy structure was sectioned during peat-cutting on Shapwick Heath, and Godwin, working along the head on a hot summer day, encountered an adder sunning itself beside the track; thus the Viper's track got its name. Part was excavated by Stephen Dewar who wrote the only detailed description we have of a structure of planks and brushwood with plaited brushwood stringers, and very heavy posts driven in pairs alongside the track and perforated to carry transverse rods across the track. When one of us (J. M. C.) first worked in the Levels, a thin strip of high peat carrying the small-gauge peat railway contained a final small section of the Viper's track but within a year or so it had been totally removed from the whole peat-cutting area.

fig. 30

Dewar and Godwin also detected and examined adjacent tracks in the immediate area, but these too were soon removed entirely, leaving by 1962 only a few heads of peat barely high enough to contain the remnants of these structures, which were radiocarbon dated to *c.* 700–600 bc. All lay immediately below fen peat with giant sedge predominant, and this horizon was correlated by Godwin to the major episode of flooding which he had identified as marking the climatic transition from Sub-Boreal to the rainier Sub-Atlantic.

One of the structures we examined in the early 1960s was called the Platform track, a rather unimaginative name but one which aptly described its character. Godwin had earlier detected several small, isolated mattresses of birch pegged to the raised bog by multitudes of short pegs, and carrying heavy alder poles with notched ends; he supposed these to be platforms, perhaps with screens set up in the notched poles, serving as look-outs over the nearby lagg area of the bog, or as fowling hides. These had been placed about 50 m between the two heaviest tracks in the area, as they converged upon the lagg, and the platform we excavated had a further trackway attached to it. We might presume that the area, quite obviously becoming wetter and wetter, had turned into a rich fowling source, and the heavy tracks and platforms were built to permit access into the fen, as much as across it; no trace of any of these tracks was ever noted to the north and it is probably correct to say that they never went all the way from the Poldens to the Westhay-Meare island. The lagg area to the south would also have been a difficult proposition to cross dry-footed, and Dewar always claimed he had found a single heavy structure just at the point where the Viper's and other tracks converged and joined, but he, and later we, excavated and found masses of wood which made no pattern and could only at best represent a collapsed and disarranged platform.

30 The Viper's track, based on observations by S. Dewar in 1947, shortly before its destruction by peat-cutting.

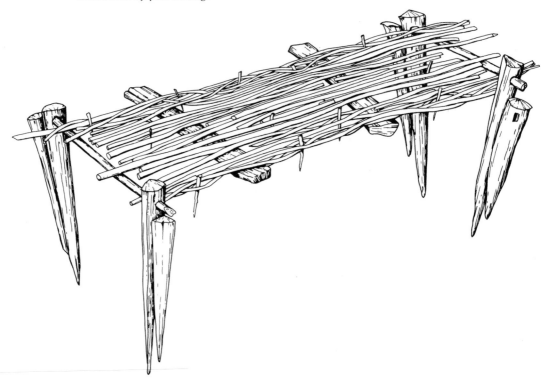

One final point concerning these structures on Meare Heath and Shapwick Heath may be worth making. Apart from their abundant evidence for woodworking in the Bronze Age, and their obvious relationship to immediate environmental changes, they hold useful information about the actual trees selected and taken by man for his structures. Dryland woods yielded oak, hazel, ash, maple and beech, supplemented by birch, alder and willow from the bog; a wide range of woods was thus available, each possessing its own character for working and use. Beech had generally been accepted as a post-Roman import on the strength of a remark by Caesar that in Britain he had found all the trees of Gaul except spruce and beech, but one of the Bronze Age tracks had a beech stake, and later on the tree was identified in a Neolithic track north of the Meare island. Godwin suggests that Caesar's *atque fagem* was probably sweet chestnut, rather than beech, and if so then Caesar was correct. Incidentally, other species also appear in our track records, although they may not have been identified in contemporary pollen; hornbeam, for example, according to pollen, was restricted to south and eastern Europe during the third millennium, and yet it is known from the Sweet Track and other structures (chapter 3).

Skinner's Wood

Our information about another Bronze Age complex even farther west at Skinner's Wood is not as complete as that from Meare Heath and Shapwick Heath. The Wood is 1100 m west of the Viper's-Nidon's track group, and 2300 m west of the Meare Heath group, and thus begins to suggest that territorial divisions may exist, each with its own complex of structures providing access into the boglands; this is discussed below.

Skinner's Wood is a small group of fields which began to be cut for peat in the late 1960s, and was searched by Colin Clements in 1970, when several slender wooden tracks were discovered. A small rodden, or extinct stream bed with mixed peat, clay and silt, was also to be seen at a high level in the peat. From the stream, fragments of a late Iron Age decorated pot were retrieved, but the trackways appeared to be lower in the peat. In 1970, we were beginning to record the Sweet Track only 750 m away from Skinner's Wood, and we managed to retrieve several wooden artifacts just as they were being scraped away by a bulldozer, as well as digging out a couple of ash posts; one of these gave a date *c.* 700 bc, linking the Skinner's Wood complex to the same time-range as the other groups farther east on Shapwick and Meare Heaths. The objects recovered were a finely worked truncheon or ridged peg of hazel and a rather neat tent-peg of maple, not in themselves very exciting but providing hints that the peats here might contain the occasional remnant of activities taking place near the base of the Polden slopes only 200 m away. Five years later, on a routine walk, our field archaeologist Janet Leng noticed a piece of roundwood in section and an immediate excavation by a small party

plate 60

plate 59   uncovered a very unusual object, a wooden fork of hazel, about 1.5 m long
from its truncated handle to the ends of the two tines. The piece had begun as a
hazel stem with one forking branch, which had then been almost completely
worked over and axed into shape, having many slightly scooped facets on the
handle as well as on the two tines which were made of the branch and the
upper part of the straight stem. The artifact was broken into fifteen pieces, and
no wonder, as the 2-tonne peat-cutting machine had passed directly over it
with only 10 cm of wet peat as cushion. Peat from around the fork was dated
c. 1400 bc. The implement was examined carefully for wear, before
conservation. The tines were D-sectioned, with a curved underside and a
flattened upper surface, and one was worn near its tip more heavily than the
other. The flattened surface of the tines was not very worn, and we therefore
presume that the fork was used to lift and perhaps throw some light material
such as grass, hay or reed. By its position in the marsh, reeds seem a likely
candidate for the fork.

A year later, Skinner's Wood was still being cut and rows of mumps were
drying beside the heads. A former peat-cutter, J. Hooper, was passing by when
he noticed a crow busily pecking at a rather shiny object embedded in a mump.
plate 61   He found that the crow was attacking a group of flint flakes, some of them still
wrapped in a padding of moss and cotton-grass, with each flake separated
from the next by a thin layer of cotton-grass. As the bulbar surfaces, and
bulbar ends, all lay in a distinctly uniform arrangement, it seems that a
package of unretouched flakes had been prepared for transport and was being
carried through the marsh when for some reason it was lost. All of the twelve
flakes had cortex, and most had been used as tools, for reeds and hides
according to use-wear analysis by Andrew Brown. The peat with the flints was
dated *c.* 1800 bc.

Tinney's Ground at Sharpham

Although Dewar and Godwin were able to record finds from the upper peats in
the Shapwick and Meare Heath areas in early years, there were other areas of
peat-cutting which escaped their inspection, and there was a complete gap in
work between about 1959 and 1963 when one of us first visited the Levels.
Areas of peat-cutting to the north and east of the classic Heaths were totally
neglected until the Project was set up in 1973. Before this time, Alan Foster had
notified us that he had seen a line of stakes in a field newly being cut at
Sharpham, far to the east, and although the field in question was visited, there
was nothing to be seen. By 1973, the field (called Tinney's Ground) was being
extensively cut with forty-one heads running north–south, and when one of
our field archaeologists, Miranda Buchanan, paid a visit she noticed an
overwhelming abundance of cut ends of wood in many of the heads at the
south-west of the field. Recording began at once, and was continued for six
years by a succession of Project field-workers and summer teams of helpers,

West   East

UPPER CUT				Track		1					3		2				
LOWER CUT	7	8	10	9	8	9	10		8	7	6	5	4	5	6	7	8

0   5   10 metres

31 The sequence of peat-cuts on Tinney's Ground over seven years, and the undulating nature of the Bronze Age tracks and platforms built on a raised bog. The upper level of peat-cutting removed many segments of prehistoric wood, and many other parts lay within the top few cm of the second (lower) cut. The numbers relate to the sequence of peat-cuts.

supplemented by excavations whenever possible. Among the various archaeologists who carried the burden of recording all the finds, Rog Palmer and Stephen Coleman did particularly valuable work. The problems were considerable, and in a way sum up the detailed work that every field-worker had to face in the Levels. The fields when taken over for cutting go through the process of draining, unridding, laying-out of heads, machine-cutting, partial back-filling of heads with top impure peat scrapings, drying and stacking, expansion of heads and so on until the first level of about 1 m of peat is totally removed. Then the second level is begun and gradually the field is lowered.

fig. 31

In Tinney's Ground, the first level of cutting took ten years or so, the second level only five, and each time heads were cut there were dozens and sometimes hundreds of exposures of cut wood in the twenty-one western heads, and occasional traces in the twenty eastern heads. The wood seen in the heads lay near the bottom of the first cut, or near the top of the second cut, so often there would be nothing to see until the second cut began in 1974 when wood too deep and missed by the machine in 1963–73 was suddenly chopped through at the top of the section. Where the wood had been higher in the peat, it was gone by the time of the second cut.

plate VI

plate 62

The field was 350 m wide, and as two levels of cuts were made, and the machine width was 1 m, there were a potential 700 heads each 250 m long to inspect, several times each since drying-out often accentuates faint wet traces seen previously. In actuality, there were far fewer lengths to see, as we had missed most of the cutting of the first level, and some of the second lower level too. Nonetheless, the distances to walk and search were immense, granted that the walking in the bottom of a wet peat-cut is not easy, and moving up and out of the cuts to inspect the hundreds of thousands of mumps which always contained chopped wood was equally strenuous.

One major problem was the recording of the observations, and plotting them on a field plan. No fixed points exist in the peatfields, as ditches are deepened and widened, heads move outwards, trees are felled, fenceposts are absent, gates are non-existent in many cases, and even bridges move or are remade. At Tinney's Ground a reasonably convenient road bridge with a bench mark was demolished midway through the survey. The answer had to be a chain survey to make a large-scale plan, with each head shown at date of survey, and very regular replottings of heads as they moved outwards with each new cutting.

Several summer seasons of excavations were carried out, with many small teams of two or three persons examining short stretches of the wooden structures where they lay at the base of a cut between heads, or at the top of the peat, and where it seemed that an excavation would be fruitful; we could not examine every section in this way. As it was, within the first full year (1974) we had 160 excavations and a further hundred soon after; in 1978 we recorded over 430 sites. The system of recording had to work in these circumstances and it generally did, although on more than one occasion a team would be sent out to dig a particular exposure, armed with field plan, tape and tools, only to miscount the head or the distance and return with an excavation report of a site not previously suspected to exist! We must have neglected or missed many potential sightings of wooden structures, but even so we managed to accumulate hundreds of records by the end of cutting on Tinney's Ground, and most of the major alignments could be picked up in at least twenty or *fig. 32* thirty places along the heads. The field plan shows all of the clear sightings in the heads, and it is apparent that various alignments existed here. Only one will be described, but basically the plan shows the existence of a number of trackways running from south-west to north-east for 100–150 m, and sometimes interconnecting, before dying out and ending midway across the present field. To the south and east there were dozens of small patches of wood which did not form clear lines or shapes. Almost all of these lay at or near the same level in the peat, and this suggests that they were broadly contemporary and represent efforts by communities to establish and maintain a safe passage across a very wet raised bog from a settlement to the south-west out towards the river Brue which flowed 500–800 m away from the tracks' ends. The tracks and patches were laid upon a wet, undulating surface of *Sphagnum* moss, cotton-grass, heather and other bog plants, and as the peats are rather pale in colour, and unhumified, the bog surface was probably very wet.

Pollen samples taken through the track structures show clear indications of a wet bog, but there are also dryland plants represented which demonstrate that cultivated land was nearby, and both plantain and cereal pollens were present in quantities which suggest quite intensive clearance and mixed arable-pasture lands on the slopes of the Sharpham peninsula some 500 m to the south-west. One of the tracks may be seen in a ditch 100 m to the west, thus within 400 m of the Sharpham slopes. Beetle studies from the tracks also point conclusively, we think, to the presence of a vigorous settlement on the peninsula. A detailed analysis by Girling of the insects from the track called Tin A shows the presence not only of beetles of an acid bog (such as *Plateumaris discolor*, a cotton-grass inhabitant, and *Locmaea suturalis*, a

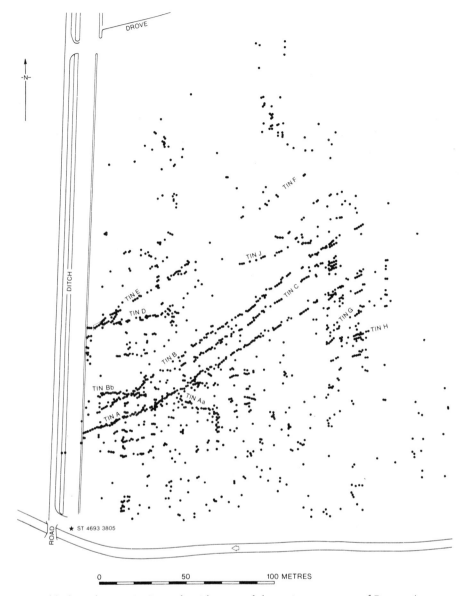

32 *Field plan of Tinney's Ground, with most of the major exposures of Bronze Age brushwood shown, and certain alignments of tracks indicated. This field plan was drawn from a series of plans made as the field was systematically trenched and lowered by machines over a period of seven years. Well over 1000 excavations and sections were recorded.*

denizen of ling), but also of seven species of dung beetles (like *Aphodius sordidus*) which signify the likely presence of herbivorous animals on the track, and thus animal husbandry on the dry grazing slopes of the peninsula.

The various lines of the major tracks shown represent a minimum number of known linear structures, yet several intersections are clear. These are places where a track either came in from the west as one and divided into two separate eastern lines, or where two lines from the west came together and went eastwards as one. The fact that most were thin brushwood tracks, made of bundles of alder dumped to form a walkway, meant that they would soon be squashed down into the wet bog surface, and overwhelmed by moss and cotton-grass, soon therefore to be replaced (perhaps even annually) by a new line of dumped bundles. In such circumstances there could be accidental overlaps and new alignments, but the junctions are evidence for the deliberate combining or dividing of paths.

plate 63

Track Tin A demonstrates all of the common, and some unusual, features of the Tinney's tracks. It was traced for 200 m, by a total of 118 separate observations and several large excavations. It had been built in three phases, the first of which attempted to stabilize the bog surface with a dense spread of alder, hazel and willow roundwood, slats, chips and fragments of oak timber, with pegs of roundwood or oak slats driven through the heaps into the bog beneath. This was a beast to excavate, with many an archaeological finger temporarily separated from its nail by a splinter, especially bark. After an interval, and because of increased wetness on the bog, the track had to be strengthened and raised; oak planks gathered from the settlement were brought to the site and heaped where the track had subsided; beside these were driven heavy posts and pegs, to try to keep planks in place but mainly to firm the surface of the bog. Over all this, the builders placed bundles of brushwood, tramped them down, heaped more on top, pegged beside and through the brushwood, and thus raised the level by a full 20 cm. Since this track was built outwards from the west, as shown both by overlapping planks and by brushwood, the bog surface varied from wet to less wet, and the plank layer was not always present. The track divided into two separate lines about 50 m from our first sighting, thus perhaps 550 m or so from its starting place; upon excavation we found that it existed in two phases: an early one providing a T-junction with the main track and a later one forming more of a forked junction. Farther to the east the track had not encountered such problems with wetness, and the first construction had survived and been in use throughout the short life of the track. Radiocarbon dates put this at *c.* 1100 bc and we think the bog may have overwhelmed Tin A finally after about ten to twenty years.

plate 65

plate 64

plate 66

The majority of tracks in Tinney's Ground were made only of brushwood, without planks, but at least one other track, Tin D, had oak which Morgan could show was contemporary with the oak from Tin A, so these two, built about 50 m apart, were probably in use at the same time. Alder, growing around the lagg between the bog and the Sharpham slope, was the dominant wood used, but the builders obviously needed all the brushwood they could get, and they felled birch, willow and bog myrtle from the drier bog surfaces, and brought in hazel, ash, alder buckthorn, yew and viburnum to supplement the alder. It will be obvious from all we have said previously that the working of wood could be carried out by breaking, tearing, chopping or slicing, using

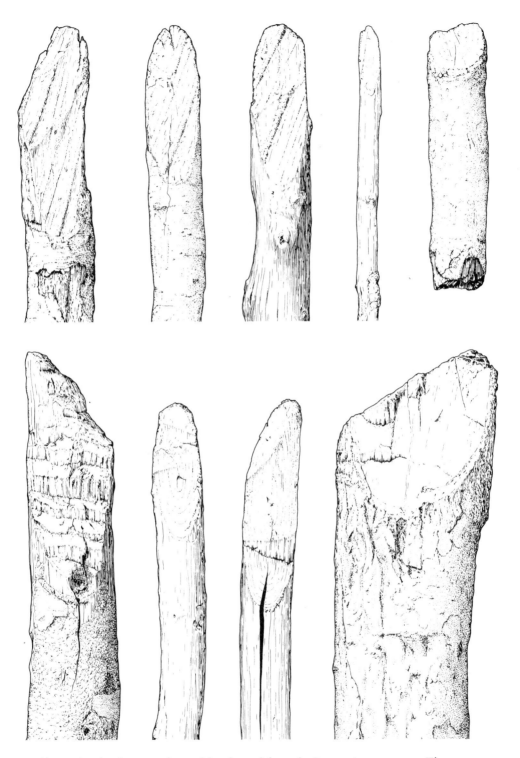

33 *Chopped ends of pegs, stakes and brushwood from the Bronze Age structures. The facets are generally smooth and sharply defined, with clear facet-junctions. Several pieces were cut by axes with damaged blades, which left ridges or grooves on the wood; these are the signatures of particular blades. Scale 1:2.*

hands, feet or various tools. The Tinney's Ground tracks contained thousands upon thousands of prepared pieces of wood, both stems and branches, as well as split timber, and we were able to record only a matter of hundreds and conserve less. Even so, this area has provided the most abundant evidence for Bronze Age axework on roundwood in Britain. The felling of trees was followed by their separation into thick roundwood for posts, pegs and heavier brushwood, with more slender branches broken or slashed into usable lengths of about 1 m. The axes used were sharp, and many slender pieces were cut through by a single blow delivered at a rather shallow angle to the stem, forming a single long facet to a sharp edge. Heavier pieces were often attacked in the same way but generally the blade did not cut completely through, and a further blow was delivered downstem of the first, so that a point was produced

plate 67   bearing several stepped facets. Where the axe blade failed to cut through, its curvature was reflected in the step up to the next facet, and so we can tell that the axes were shallowly and evenly curved, and had rather flat blades which left only slightly dished facets. Larger stems used for posts were chopped from several sides, to make a pencil-like point.

Among the many hundreds of chopped pieces are a small number which have facets with various ridges and grooves in the wood. These are the marks

fig. 33   left by axes which had imperfect blades, bearing either a slight gouge or a small piece of metal bent away from the main smooth edge. Each axe will have its own signature, and it is thus possible to say that particular pieces of wood were cut with an individual axe. At least ten different axes were used for the tracks, and the two tracks already related by tree-ring studies (Tin A and Tin D) also have wood cut with the same axe, a welcome confirmation for tree-rings. These 'signed' axes further allow us to deduce the exact manner of working. One piece, for example, has three facets and the top facet has a reverse set of ridges compared with those of the middle and lower facets; the axeman had begun to cut this piece by holding it vertically and backhanding it down, he then turned it more obliquely to the ground and axed with a forehand stroke, finishing the job with a final swipe at the tip which just picked up part of the ridging, all presumably in the space of about five seconds.

The tracks at Tinney's Ground, allied to the pollen and beetle evidence, suggest intensive clearance of trees and farming on the Sharpham peninsula. From the settlement, the rich resources of the bog and the river Brue were reached by the tracks built over the lagg and up the rand of the bog, thereafter following a more level course eastwards towards the river. Nearing the river, there have been reports of a structure, cut away at a high level in the peats before 1965, and traces of two heavy platforms.

Bronze Age communities

Our work in the upper peats of the Levels has therefore identified four areas along the Polden Hills where later Bronze Age settlements existed, from

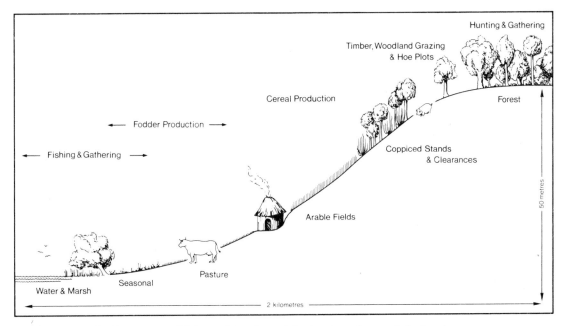

34 *The concave landscape: a model for prehistoric exploitation in and around the Levels.*

Sharpham in the east, through Meare Heath and Shapwick Heath to Skinner's Wood. Each of these had its own woodland, pasture and arable fields. The upland woods provided oak timber, coppiced hazel stands, pannage for pigs, and wild animals to hunt. The well-drained slopes were often cultivated for cereal and other crops. Farther down, cattle grazed, moving upland during the winter, and down onto the sweet meadows near the bog edge in the summer months when the floods of winter had receded. The wet bog, with its pools and sluggish streams, would here and there provide opportunities for fishing and eeling, and excellent wildfowling as a seasonal exercise; there would also be regular collection of edible or otherwise useful wild plants such as moss, *fig. 34* cotton-grass, and ling, and sedges and reeds from different parts of the wetland. The whole system would have furnished the variety and alternatives that were an insurance against particular disasters, such as the failure of cereals, or persistence of floods, or absence of migrant wildfowl.

Each of the areas where this kind of economy was practised is separated from its neighbour(s) by about 1500 m of hillslope and bogland, but there is one gap on Walton Heath where our first work encountered Neolithic peats and from where there are no certain traces. However, signs of activity of the late second and early first millennium bc have been found at Stileway, due north of Walton Heath on the eastern edge of Meare island; these may represent one end of a long-lost route to the south. The settlements, identified *fig. 35* by their own sets of trackways, Skinner's Wood, Shapwick Heath, Meare Heath, possibly Walton Heath, and the Sharpham peninsula, would thus

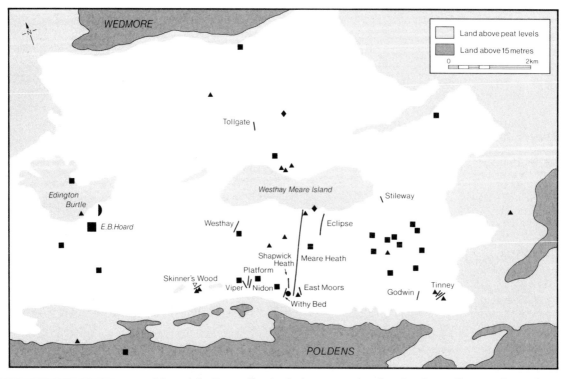

35 Map of the Brue valley in the later second and earlier first millennium bc, with major track lines and other finds shown. The known position of these tracks suggests a well-ordered system of movement in the raised boglands, probably devised by the four or five communities settled along the lower Polden slopes.

- ■ bronze
- ● pottery
- ▲ flint
- ▽ wooden fork
- ◆ amber
- ❱ yew bow

appear to have controlled not only their Polden territories but also transects across the bog to sister-settlements or farmsteads on the island, or to the opportunities offered by the sprawling river Brue.

There are a number of problems associated with this model, among them the vexed one of chronology and flooding. Godwin clearly demonstrated that his Meare Heath and Shapwick Heath tracks were built upon a wet raised bog soon to be inundated by floodwaters from the base-rich slopes around the Levels. This major flooding is dated *c*. 700 bc and thus suits some of the trackways, but not all. The Tinney's tracks are much earlier in date, *c*. 1100 bc, and the Meare Heath track itself was built perhaps a century or so before the flooding horizon identified above it, and in human terms this is a long time.

Should we accept that the floods when they came were climatically induced when there is no universal evidence for such a firm and dated horizon? The answer is not simple and must involve several factors. Among these is the character of the raised bog itself, which after all holds the flooding evidence in its *Cladium* peats. We know that raised bogs develop slowly from a small central point when waterlogging is due to rain-derived acidic water rather than base-rich ground water, and acid-preferring plants such as moss and cotton-grass thrive. Dating of the bog sequences in the Levels suggests that the raised bog developed near the centre of the Levels, on the Westhay Levels, and spread slowly towards the Poldens, with the island of Westhay-Meare holding up its progress so that the fens and fenwoods of Shapwick and Meare Heaths were overwhelmed 100–200 years later. Once established, the raised bog was vigorous and grew upwards to a great thickness of as much as 8 m in places on Shapwick Heath. When floodwaters arrived, they did not necessarily overtop the highest parts of the raised bog, which maintained its acidic regime only influenced in part by the surrounding base-rich floodwaters. Thus the characteristic *Cladium* flooding horizons in the raised bog peats would be unevenly represented, of variable thickness, and only thinly represented or not at all in some of the peats of the early first millennium bc.

The reasons behind the flooding are also likely to contribute, we think, to an uneven representation. Far from a simple climatic deterioration which brought increased rainfall, and thus run-off, to the area, there are complex local topographic and anthropogenic factors responsible for the flooding. As we have seen in chapter 1, the drainage pattern of the Levels is volatile, with such shallow gradients to the rivers that only slight changes in land and sea or alterations in sand dune formation will cause back-up waters to invade the land. There is evidence for such silt-laden waters invading the valley of the Brue in the last centuries of the first millennium bc and possibly earlier. The Brue itself has had a varied existence, its early line running northwards from Glastonbury through the Godney Narrows and onto Godney Moor, thence through the Bleadney Gap and into the River Axe (chapters 7 and 8). To the west, across the great peatbogs of all the Moors, Heaths and Levels, there was no natural drainage of the land, and ponding and flooding were endemic, the waters only slowly and tortuously finding a way across, through and around the raised bogs to a few exits, including the Brue. The landscape was thus prone to flooding at all times, and up to recent years the winter months were characterized by inundation of the major parts of the land. But what might have caused the prolonged flooding horizons of the first millennium bc? Blocked exits would hold back the drainage of the bogs, and bring in base-rich waters from the upper Brue, but we suspect another factor was at work, the influence of man on the vegetation of the hillslopes and islands. We know that intensive clearances were underway all along the Poldens, and on the islands too, and these would certainly have increased the run-off of base-rich waters into the lagg, thereby adding yet more water to an already choked system. It is thus a combination of factors, climatic perhaps, topographical and human certainly, which created conditions of major flooding from time to time in various parts of the Levels; some areas withstood inundation by reason of height or position within the complicated local landscape. There is a further potential factor, as we have seen in chapter 4: the beaver, which could cause widespread flooding over large areas. One bogland investigated by us in

Canada had been flooded by beaver for 6000 years. Could this animal have contributed to local severe flooding in parts of the Levels?

When we speak of the Bronze Age in Britain, we are generally concerned with burials, pottery and metalwork. Here in the Levels we have not had these advantages and instead must concentrate on just the kinds of evidence lacking from most other Bronze Age sites. There are no known round barrows in the Levels, the nearest cemeteries being those of the Quantocks and the Mendips so well studied by Leslie Grinsell; these are over 10 km away from the Polden Hills upon which there are very few traces of Bronze Age burials of any sort, or pottery or metalwork. Pottery of the Bronze Age is rather rare in the Levels, but as it is mostly funerary on the Mendips and Quantocks its absence may reflect the lack of burials. However, potsherds in the acid peats are not likely to survive well, and those few vessels we have recovered on Meare Heath were soggy and difficult to recognize; peat-cutters would be unlikely to identify such fragments, and would much prefer to find bronze axes and the like. Most of the cutters have been happy to hand in flints, stone axes, wooden and metal objects, only professing that if gold is found, they will keep it.

There are quite fundamental problems involved in trying to relate the evidence from the Levels for sophisticated woodland management and technologies with the presumed equally tenacious and evolved craftsmanship of the occupations on the uplands to north and south-west. Burials of Beaker and Early Bronze Age character are abundant on the Mendips and on the northern Quantocks, and the henges of the Mendips are probably contemporary. Settlement sites, however, are rare, and this is reflected in the relatively sparse signs of activity in the Levels in the early second millennium bc. Yet the very abundant track- and platform-building of the late second and early first millennia bc relate to few obviously contemporary signs in the uplands, where there are rather few metalwork finds, and hardly any burials and settlements. However, the later Bronze Age occupations on hilltops at South Cadbury and Ham Hill may demonstrate the beginning of defensive and prestigious settlement hierarchies for which the Iron Age is noted. But in looking at the overall picture of activity in the boglands of the first millennium, we cannot but be impressed by its energy and wealth, perhaps indicative of a fundamental shift of emphasis from upland to lowland during the course of the second millennium bc.

Over many years of peat-cutting, bronze implements and other artifacts have often been found and we know of at least sixty Bronze Age pieces, none of them associated directly with the trackways which are remarkably devoid of small inorganic objects. These bronzes are almost all stray finds made in the peat by hand-cutters of long ago, when the upper peats were being removed, and they easily approach the quantities of bronzes recovered from the surrounding and much wider areas of the Mendips and Quantocks. It is probably significant that only one piece, a copper flat axe, is typologically of the early Bronze Age and all the others are of forms most usually dated to the

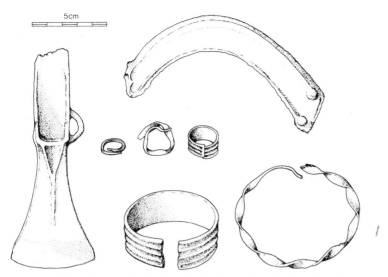

36 *Part of the Edington Burtle hoard of tools and jewels. The hoard was buried in the peat in a wooden box. Drawn by M. Rouillard.*

late second and early first millennia bc; this suits the evidence from the peats of the Levels with its rather sparse traces of early Bronze Age activity and much greater evidence for the later period. Further, most of the bronzes are axes of one sort or another – in other words, implements consonant with woodwork – rather than spearheads or swords. Of ornaments, there are none except for those in two hoards noted below, but there are a few amber beads from the peat.

There is a problem here in relating these artifacts to the trackways and platforms of the peats because, in the early decades of cutting, many finds were lost completely or, if they survived, their provenance was forgotten or disregarded. There are 7 axes, 4 spearheads, 2 blades and some fine leaf-shaped flint knives which we can record only as found before 1902 in 'turbaries west of Glastonbury'. They were collected by William Stradling who worked around Chilton Polden, a village on the western slopes of the Poldens overlooking Catcott Heath. We know that the peatlands here were being cut in the nineteenth century, and conceivably all these finds could have been made on this Heath. No Bronze Age tracks are recorded from the likely route, so well-used in the Neolithic, between the Polden Hills and the great sand island of Edington and Catcott Burtle; we suspect that all were removed in the nineteenth century when only the bronzes were saved. If so, this area of the Poldens, 3000 m to the west of the Skinner's Wood complex, adds another settlement area to the picture. There are a few certain bronzes from Catcott Heath, as well as the suspected group, and one of the most important Bronze Age hoards from southern Britain was found in a peat-cutting around 1840–50

fig. 36

just off the island at Edington Burtle. The hoard, consisting of 4 palstaves, 4 sickles and various torcs, bracelets and 3 small linked rings, lay in a wooden box squared on the outside and scooped to an oval shape within. The ornaments in the hoard are of types which were produced in the south-west of England and are firmly dated to the late second millennium bc. How they came to be deposited in a box in the peats just off the Burtle island we do not know, but Stradling in his report on the hoard was not hindered by lack of imagination: the three linked rings were a 'Jogh-Draoch, or chain-ring of divination' worn on the third finger of the left hand of a Druidess. Thus, 'might not then a British priestess, at a very early date, have lost this then most valuable cist [box] from her canoe. The knives [sickles] are precisely of the same pattern as those of gold found in Ireland, and which were supposed to have been used for sacrificing the victims in those barbarous days. The torque, armlet and rings convince us that she was one of high rank, and the Jogh-Draoch, I conceive, gave the possessor the order of priesthood.' Who knows?

44 Experiments in hurdle-making. Young shoots are being removed by stone axe from a hazel stool in a coppiced wood.

45 Felling an ash tree with Neolithic and Bronze Age axes.

46 Experiments in hurdle-making. The rods are being evenly woven around the upright sails to make a hurdle of Walton Heath size, *c.* 2 m long and 1 m high.

Opposite:

47 Conservation of a Neolithic hurdle. The isolated hurdle is being undercut, and a plywood and steel lifting platform built beneath it.

48 Conservation of a Neolithic hurdle. The hurdle, in its steel tank, is being gradually impregnated with PEG.

49 Bronze Age axes used in the experimental chopping, splitting and shaping of wood from the Levels. The hafts are modern.

Right:

50 Hazel roundwood chopped with bronze axes to duplicate the facets and ridging on pegs and brushwood from structures in the Levels. From left, a bronze flat axe, palstave, and socketed axe, were used.

51 Experimental reconstruction of the Sweet Track, with one rail in position and pegs driven across it.

52 Experimental reconstruction of the Sweet Track. One plank is already in place, forming a raised walkway at least 40 cm above the swamp, and a second rail is being pegged into the soft peats.

53 Excavations on the Meare Heath track. The structure was embedded in firm, drying peats, but the oak timbers and other elements were still well-preserved.

54 (*below left*) The Meare Heath track, upper surface, looking north. The walking surface consisted of pairs of planks laid side by side (foreground, slipped) often upon more widely spaced transverse bearers (background). In some cases the transverses were heavy beams perforated and pegged into the marsh (middle).

55 (*below right*) The Meare Heath track, lower surface, looking south. Where the bog surface was particularly wet and soft, the builders dumped brushwood and miscellaneous broken timber, to provide a foundation for the transverses and plank walkway.

56 The Meare Heath track was built in places in a heavier and more structured way, with both transverse and longitudinal timbers holding the upper plank walkway, here severely desiccated and eroded.

57 Axe facets on a heavy Bronze Age plank from Meare Heath. The facets are clean and slightly dished, with clear ridges separating each axe mark.

58 Sickle flint with gloss acquired in use, found near the Meare island terminal of the Meare Heath track.

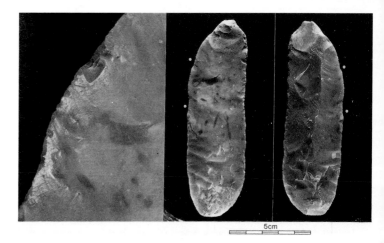

5cm

59 Bronze Age reed-fork from Skinner's Wood, Shapwick. Abandoned in the watery environs of a bog pool *c.* 1400 bc, the fork was broken by the weight of a peat-machine which had passed over it just before discovery.

60 Wooden truncheon or flanged peg, a stray find from Skinner's Wood.

61 A hoard of Bronze Age flint flakes from Skinner's Wood. The flakes had been used as cutting tools before they were packed with cotton-grass for transport. Date *c.* 1800 bc.

62 Tinney's Ground, Sharpham, an area with many Bronze Age brushwood trackways. The field had undergone peat-cutting which removed parts of many tracks, leaving other parts untouched or only sliced by the blade of the machine (note blade mark in right foreground, and total loss of brushwood in trackways behind).

63 Section through successive building phases of track Tinney's A, with wood in the mumps stacked above the head.

67 Chopped end of a brushwood piece from Tinney's Ground, *c.* 1100 bc. Eight facets survive on this piece, and the angles of entry, and curvature of the bronze blade, are clearly visible. Diameter at base 55 mm.

64–66 (*Left*) The brushwood track Tinney's A, *c.* 1100 bc. The upper walking surface consisted of bundles of brushwood dumped along the line, and pegged in along the sides and through the middle of the brushwood. The central part of the track was heavily worn. (*Below left*) The line of Tinney's A track had been set across a wet raised bog, and where conditions were particularly soft, a foundation was made from used planks, stumps and miscellaneous wood. (*Below*) The junction of two brushwood tracks at Tinney's Ground, where a main line separated into two branches heading east away from the Sharpham settlement.

The Two Counties Match Co., Honiton, Devon

Average Contents 45

Series of 20 pictures

No 8 GLASTONBURY LAKE VILLAGE

Historic Westcountry Safety Matches

68 The Glastonbury Iron Age settlement, interpreted as pile-dwellings, on a matchbox of the early twentieth century.

69 (*bottom*) Glastonbury Lake Village. Parallel logs on the far edge of the excavation form part of the collapsed palisade around the southern edge of the settlement; in the foreground are the more random timbers of the foundation.

Opposite:

70 The Causeway at Glastonbury, exposed by Bulleid in 1893. The eroded tops of three vertical planks can be seen at intervals along the edge of the rubble-capped bank to the left. One of these was located in the 1984 excavations. The vertical marker posts belong to Bulleid's grid system.

71 Excavation of part of the Causeway at Glastonbury by the Somerset Levels Project in 1984, exposing an area seen by Bulleid in 1893. The Causeway proved to be a solid but low bank of clay and rubble, edged by massive oak planks.

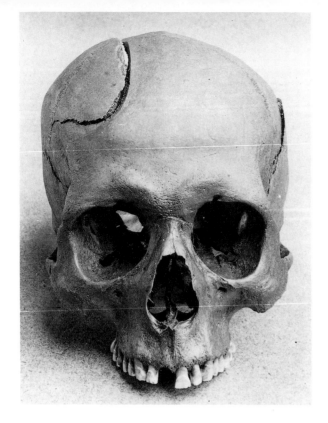

72 Human skull from Glastonbury, one of those held by Boyd-Dawkins to be evidence of a terminal massacre of the inhabitants.

73 (*bottom*) Mound 67 at Glastonbury, with hearth of lias slabs embedded in a square clay base 1.2 m across; this hearth was set off-centre in a clay floor about 4 m diameter.

Opposite:

74 Wattle-work in the Glastonbury settlement, found by Bulleid beneath Mound 56. The spacing of the split oak sails was similar to the spacing of the holes in the timber just to the left of the hurdles, suggesting that the wattle-work was collapsed walling, once held upright in the 'break'.

75 Decorated clay hearth from Glastonbury.

76 Excavation at Meare Village by Bulleid and Gray. One of the few large expanses of timber is exposed beneath the clay mounding, capped on the right by a stone platform.

77 Meare Village West, 1979 excavation by the Somerset Levels Project. Each polythene bag contains one or more finds from the occupation floor, and the yield from only a few hours' work is shown here.

78 Wood from Glastonbury, photographed shortly after excavation by Bulleid and Gray. These are five of the ash and oak pieces thought by Bulleid to be 'parts of looms or appliances for making textile fabric'.

79 Glastonbury Lake Village. Iron blades, excavated and photographed by Bulleid and Gray. Preservation of iron was not good on the sites of Glastonbury and Meare. Scale in inches.

80 Excavation by wooden spatula in the soft peats along the Sweet Track, with a finely flaked flint arrowhead emerging, unmoved since it fell into the reed swamp c. 6000 years ago.

81 Open Day on the Sweet Track. Compare plate 8. By such events, the work of the Project and the problems of the Levels can be explained to local groups and other visitors.

82 The Museum of the Somerset Levels. Via photographs, drawings, and artifacts, both peat-cutting and archaeological finds are displayed.

7 Iron Age conflicts: the settlements of Glastonbury and Meare

Radiocarbon
Calibration

0bc   0bc

500   500

            1000
1000
            1500

1500
            2000

2000   2500

            3000
2500
            3500

3000
            4000
            CALIBRATED
3500
UNCALIBRATED

I'm got plenty to go by, to form my own opinion of what happened, whenever it happened, and I don't agree altogether with any o' the authorities I'm been talking about.

(S. Marshall, *Fenland Chronicle*, Cambridge 1967)

The ponderous, flapping flight of a white-tailed sea eagle would drive the mallard, the little teal, the colourful scaup and the red-breasted merganser to take shelter, but whooper swans had size and strength for protection, as had the flocks of pelican and of crane. Seaward, the cormorant and puffin would dive, the one under water and the other into nesting burrows, as the eagle flew overhead. But the eagle's preference was for fish, and a shallow, noisy plunge into the lake might win the predator a roach, perch, shad or trout. Otter and beaver were probably safe from the eagle, but not from man, and they together with all the waterfowl and fish, and the eagle too, fell victim to the people of the Levels in the late first millennium bc. Their bones, preserved at the settlements of Glastonbury and Meare, give us a first indication of the environment within reach of these Iron Age villages, with large expanses of shallow freshwater, fringed with dense beds of reed and sedge and interrupted by occasional patches of fen woodland. Moorland birds, such as the black grouse, show raised bog ever-present, and the puffins and cormorants suggest a not-too-distant coastline. However, the animal bones from a settlement site cannot be used for a detailed reconstruction of purely local environment, since we do not know how far people ranged when hunting, fishing and fowling. For greater precision, we must turn to the plant evidence and the sequence of natural deposits outside the inhabited areas.

Immediately the picture of the wetland conditions becomes extremely complex. In the 1940s and 50s, Godwin made several sequences of borings in the region of the historic Meare Pool (see chapter 2) to investigate the origin and fluctuations of the pool, and its relationship to the Iron Age settlements. He established that a large area to the immediate north of the Meare-Westhay *fig. 37* island had not progressed through the classic vegetational sequence of reed swamp, fenwood and raised bog, as seen on Shapwick Heath. Instead, the area had remained much wetter, with expanses of open water, dense beds of *Phragmites* and *Cladium*, occasional birch and willow, and loose mats of floating hypnoid mosses which from time to time supported a development of

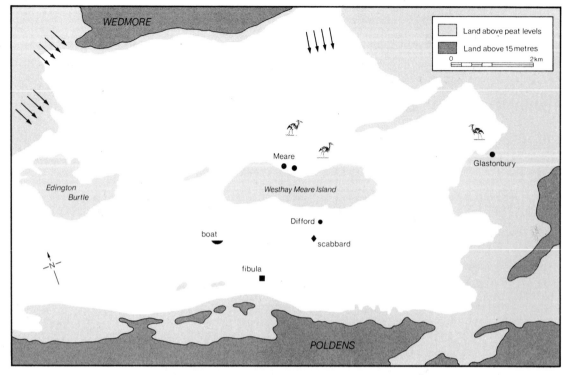

37 *The Brue valley in the later first millennium bc. Meare Pool lies in the area occupied by the two wading birds, and the single bird is in the shallow waters surrounding the Glastonbury settlement.*

raised bog, rafted out over the water. When Glastonbury and Meare were occupied, Godwin suggested that raised bogs were well-developed to the west, and spread widely over the former open water of Meare Pool, with the Meare settlement placed on their margin. Open water was not far to the east, and open water surrounded the Glastonbury settlement, but there may have been further raised bog, spreading up from the south-east corner of Meare island and separating the reedy Meare waters from those of Glastonbury. From east to west, the wetland environment therefore changed from shallow mere to reedy marsh to the spongy moors of raised bog.

The river Brue did not then run in its present course, nor did Godwin's borings locate any other channel draining to the west, but he remained uncertain of the Iron Age course of the Brue. He inferred that it flowed through the eastern end of the area, bringing in the supplies of freshwater that prevented any development of raised bog, and then flowing north either to pass through the Bleadney Gap and join the Axe, or to run westwards along the southern slopes of the Wedmore ridge. In the early Middle Ages, before the proto-Water Authority diversions of the Abbots of Glastonbury, the course of the Brue undoubtedly ran north to join the Axe, but when it first flowed this way is still unclear.

Our own work on the two Iron Age settlements is not yet completed, but pollen and beetle analyses from a number of sites around Meare island show that towards the end of the first millennium bc there was a general increase in forest clearance and expansion of herbs. The increase marks the opening of regional Pollen Zone G, the final zone in the sequence established by Beckett and Hibbert. Variations from one pollen diagram to another show that dryland conditions were not uniform, and the general picture of a sudden increase in clearance is modified by evidence for the regeneration of elm on the south side of Meare island more or less when the northern edge was being cleared and the settlement on the raised bog was initiated. Moreover, the woodland being cleared was secondary growth, of fairly poor quality judging by the tree-ring patterns of the wood recovered from our excavations at Meare, and perhaps only forming patchy and fairly open cover since light-demanding shrubby species, such as elder and alder buckthorn, were abundant. Put together, the plant evidence indicates a mosaic of fields and woodland covering Meare island, passing through stages of cultivation, regeneration, exploitation for fuel and construction timber, and renewed clearing throughout the last centuries of the first millennium bc and into the Romano-British period. The plant evidence for clearance and cultivation on Meare island is reinforced by the identification of beetle species which inhabit meadows or cultivated areas, including *Bembidion properans* and *Dromius linearis*, and dung beetles indicate the local presence of herbivores.

The sea was not far from the settlements, as sea eagle and puffin remind us, and at some stage tidal waters were to deposit the marine clay that spread through the Bleadney Gap to within a stone's throw of the Glastonbury settlement. Exactly when this occurred is uncertain, but the location of salt-workings gives a further clue to the coastline, and shows that, in the Iron Age, saltwater may have reached inland up the Axe to the edge of the Wedmore hills, while the numerous mounds around the northern edge of Edington Burtle probably result from Romano-British salt-workings. In the closing centuries BC and the early centuries AD, saltwater came closer to Meare island than it had done for many centuries.

The settlements of Glastonbury and Meare were probably established when the surrounding environment was at its most diverse both in the wetlands and on dryland. Within a 10-km radius the inhabitants could have found salt and brackish waters, tidal estuaries, reed swamp and shallow lakes, freshwater rivers, fen woodland and great expanses of raised bog, dryland forest at various stages of growth, some of it coppiced, and soils of sandy burtle and of lias island to cultivate or graze. The landscape rose from open water and raised bog, through island and ridge, to the high points of Glastonbury Tor and Brent Knoll and up the Mendip scarp with its caves and gorges to the plateau beyond.

Early excavations

Our knowledge of the Glastonbury and Meare settlements depends heavily on the work of Arthur Bulleid and Harold St. George Gray. Bulleid's discovery of Glastonbury in 1892 has already been described (chapter 2) and the enthusiasm and dedication which lay behind that discovery continued through half a century of further exploration and excavation. Virtually the whole of the

fig. 38 Glastonbury settlement was exposed in seven summer seasons from 1892 to 1898, and a further four seasons from 1904 to 1907. Funds for the excavation were raised from many sources. General Pitt-Rivers gave £5 and Robert Munro 2 guineas, the Society of Antiquaries contributed £20, and the British Association made eight donations totalling £277.10s. 'Entrance fees to the Field' brought in £92.18s.6d and the Excavation Fund eventually totalled £696.19s. The widespread interest in the site expressed by the list of donors is manifest also in those who contributed to the publication, amongst them many museums and libraries including Harvard University Library and the Royal Library, Copenhagen. Glastonbury featured in the *Illustrated London News*,

plate 68 and even, as a village of pile-dwellings, on the boxes of the Honiton Match Company. The interest of the site attracted the advice and services of eminent prehistorians and scientists. Munro and Boyd Dawkins both visited the excavations and contributed to the publication, Munro writing a survey of European lake-settlements and Boyd Dawkins identifying and discussing the human and other mammal bone. Clement Reid identified the cereals and other seeds recovered, and C. W. Andrews of the British Museum identified the bird bones.

In 1911, the first volume of the excavation report was published and by 1917 the second and final volume was out. The volumes set a standard of clarity, illustration, and wide range of post-excavation studies that was admirable for the time, and is not always matched today. They have provided the basis for several significant re-interpretations of the site, and for the account of Glastonbury which is given here. We are happy to rely heavily on the observations of Bulleid and Gray, and particularly on Bulleid's comments on peat and wood, for wherever we have been able to check them in the field the conclusions drawn some seventy-five years ago have been borne out by our present techniques of investigation. The shortfall that we notice now is not in the accuracy of the observations, but in the detailed description of the stratigraphy of the settlement and the context of finds. These are factors which limit re-interpretation, but not to the extent that none can be attempted.

Glastonbury

The Glastonbury settlement was built in that area of the Levels where open water had always predominated, broken by occasional patches of willow and alder and reeds. The village was built on one such patch, using the felled trees as part of the foundation of a gigantic crannog, gigantic in the sense that most

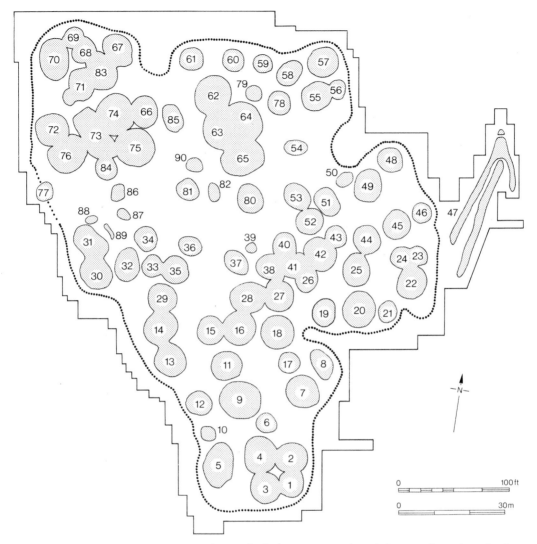

38 Glastonbury Lake Village, as planned by Bulleid, showing mounds and their numbers, the palisade (dotted line) and the extent of the excavated area. Mound 47 outside the palisade is in fact the Causeway with its underlying embankment.

contemporary crannogs in northern Britain and Ireland supported only a couple of houses, whereas Glastonbury was to comprise upwards of eighty structures. To east and north, across water, lay the dry grounds of modern Glastonbury and Godney, to south and west the lake was bordered by raised bog, beyond which lay the reedy Meare Pool and Meare island, and further expanses of heather, moss and cotton-grass. Somewhere flowed the Brue, perhaps past the eastern edge of the settlement; we prefer to think, however, that the extent of open water and the sluggishness of drainage meant that no single river channel was evident, merely a general drift of current up from the south-east and northwards round the village.

The foundations of the artificial island were made of brushwood and larger trunks, including the locally felled willow and alder mentioned above. Alder predominated, a sensible choice for wood that was to be permanently waterlogged, because it rots less than other species in such conditions. Ash and oak were also found, and must have been carried in from drier ground, as was the bracken, rubble and clay used to pack the foundations. Bulleid refers to peat being used to fill up holes, especially around the edge of the village just inside the palisade, where the logs were carefully arranged in layers set at right angles to each other.

plate 69 The palisade was a substantial affair of solid, upright logs, sometimes several rows thick, which entirely surrounded the village but for one break of about 18 m in the western edge. The majority of the logs were alder, with some birch and oak and other species, and they were 7–23 cm in diameter and 1.5–4.0 m long, with a sharpened lower end. The full height of the palisade is uncertain, as any exposed upper portion would have weathered and broken at ground level, but Bulleid suggested an original height sufficient to protect the village as well as to retain or contain the foundation deposits, which was undoubtedly one function of the wall of upright logs. Further strength was given to the structure by weaving more slender rods in and out of the uprights, producing a sort of coarse hurdle-work.

The gap in the western edge was filled in part at least by a low bank of placed peat, about 1 m high and 2 m wide. It was reinforced by a central row of large posts and an outer row of more slender posts bound together with wattle-work. On the eastern edge of the village, outside the palisade, two further artificial banks were built, running out from the settlement. One consisted of clay, timber and brushwood capped by a thin layer of rubbly lias and edged with walls of carefully finished oak planks. This bank, which Bulleid called a

plate 70 Causeway, was about 45 m long and 2 m wide, and beneath it was a second mound, Bulleid's Embankment, built mainly of lias blocks with stretches of timber and hurdle retaining walls. It has generally been thought that the Causeway led out from the village to a landing-stage at its river end. In late 1984, we carried out three small excavations at Glastonbury, around the periphery of the settlement, and one of these unexpectedly exposed a part of

plate 71 the Causeway. We had assumed that Bulleid had removed it all when he excavated in this area in 1893, but although he exposed all the Causeway, he sectioned it and the Embankment in one place only. Thanks to his photographs and plan, we were able to tie in our excavations exactly with that of ninety years earlier, even to the identification of a particular plank. Our observations left us unconvinced that the narrow, low bank had served as a causeway, but we thought it might have anchored a substantial wooden superstructure, a raised walkway perhaps; in other words, the Causeway held the vertical planks in place rather than the planks retaining the Causeway.

Back within the palisade was the village, a collection of buildings set upon clay floors, loosely grouped into four or five main areas, with open spaces and paths between. Questions of chronology and the function and contemporaneity of the buildings are difficult to elucidate, because of the paucity of stratigraphic detail; several interpretations have been put forward, and will be examined below. Less problematic are the detailed observations made of surviving elements of the structures, and these will be considered first. They offer much in the way of organic evidence to bulk out our dryland knowledge of Iron Age buildings.

No two buildings from Glastonbury were identical, but the general pattern can be determined. They were circular, with a thick clay floor, vertical wattle   plate 74
and daub wall, and a fairly wide entrance; inside was a round raised hearth, and the central post to carry the roof, which was probably thatched. Evidence from individual mounds fills out the picture. The mounds themselves were the product of superimposed clay floors, renewed up to ten times as the floors sank into the soft, damp ground. The clay, which was imported from at least 1 km away, was laid down in a layer 5 to 65 cm thick, originally flat and smooth but liable to sink where the substructure was weak, and later where great weight   fig. 39
accumulated above. Care was taken to level up the floors, whether filling in slight depressions with new clay, or adding timber to build up a bad dip before a new floor was laid. In eight mounds, traces of wooden floorboards 15–20 cm wide were found, relatively well-preserved examples coming from floors ii, iii and iv of Mound 27 where parallel boards had been put on the clay surface. In Mounds 4 and 45, the boards were arranged in concentric circles parallel to the walls rather than to each other. All floor and Mound numbers are those given by Bulleid.

The walls were made of wattle and daub on a strong post framework. The posts were 5–22 cm in diameter, and seem to have been driven through the clay floor near its edge, rather than straight into the peat just beyond it. They were set 15–40 cm apart, and rods were woven in and out of them, to make a wattle wall that was then covered with daub. Mound 4 had a clear ring of wall posts, and a little wattle preserved, whereas Mound 13 (to be described below) had an almost-complete circle of wattle-work. Mounds 14 and 16 produced daub. The height of the walls is uncertain; Bulleid suggested 2 m, on the basis of preserved hurdles found horizontal in the substructure, but there is no need to   plate 74
suppose 2 m as standard, particularly since the circular walls were woven *in situ*.

Details of roofing are less certain. Burnt rushes, found amongst the debris of several buildings which had caught fire, might have come from a thatched roof, and given the local abundance of *Phragmites* and *Cladium*, the use of one of these excellent thatching materials is possible. Some but not all mounds had one or more central posts which may have supported the roof; the fairly large building on Mound 35 had two central oak posts, but it is not clear whether they were in use together. The evidence from Mound 9, on the other hand, is sufficiently detailed to suggest replacement of the central post on some occasions of reflooring and rebuilding the walls.

As the posts appear to have been set very close to or right against the raised hearths that were often found near the centre of the clay floors, it is possible that their function related to the hearths rather than to the roof.

fig. 39

The evidence for doorways indicates a wide opening, 1.2–2.1 m across. Some care was taken to make the floor strong where people were passing in and out. In Mound 29, which had only a slight brushwood foundation, the entrance to the building was reinforced with two layers of timber, projecting about 60 cm outside the walls and 1.5 m within. Mound 74, which had a very solid and carefully laid alder-log foundation, had a 1.8 m gap in its wall; here an elaborate arrangement of horizontal beams in three layers flanked by two rows of vertical posts, suggests a porch with reinforced floor, although most of the floor structure lies within the building and was overlain by the alder logs and then by clay. In several cases the entrance was paved, as in Mound 45 where an area about 1.2 × 1.8 m, outside the walls, was paved with lias slabs and bordered on the inside edge with a piece of timber. Mound 23, immediately south of Mound 45, had an area of neat paving just outside a 1.5 m gap in the walls, but no timber sill.

It seems from the above examples that timber reinforcement was placed mostly at an entrance and within, under the clay floors, whereas stone reinforcement was placed at an entrance and without, on the exposed surface. No actual doors were found *in situ*. Bulleid suggested the use of solid wood, or of hurdle-work. It seems that whatever filled the gap was generally attached to the wall posts, except in a few cases where the terminal posts were replaced by squared oak planks, as in Mounds 9 and 13.

plate 73

Many hearths were found at Glastonbury, carefully built raised platforms usually of clay and usually circular. They were commonly 1.0–1.2 m in diameter, and a few centimetres thick, with a sloping or a bevelled edge. They were renewed more frequently than the floors. Floor iv of Mound 30, for example, had seven successive hearths, one on top of the other and separated by thin layers of ash. But floors ii and iii of the same mound and many other floors had but one hearth each. In addition to clay, hearth platforms of gravel, gravel and clay mix, rubble and stone slabs were found. It may be that the different materials reflected different uses of the hearths, as might the variations in the shape of the edge. Mound 9 had a rectangular clay hearth

plate 75

decorated with circles, and one wonders if this was not intended for some altogether different use. An oven was also found in Mound 9, as in Mounds 4 and 37. These were sunk about 25 cm deep into the floor, 75 cm in diameter, and found full of ash and bits of baked clay which were taken to be pieces of the fallen sides. The terms 'hearth' and 'oven' are Bulleid's, used because of the associated evidence for burning and for ash and charcoal.

The size of the buildings varied from mound to mound, and was liable to increase with each rebuilding. Where wall evidence was preserved, the

Mound 74

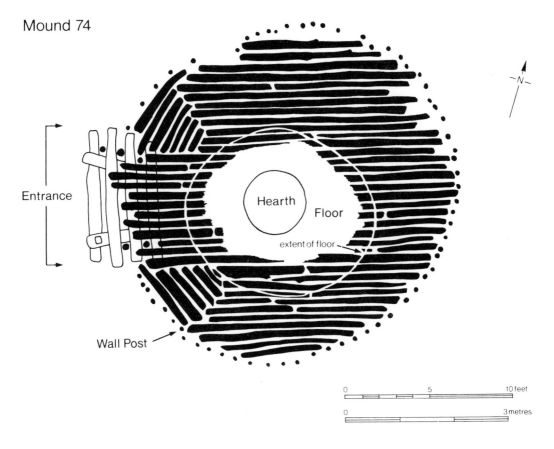

Entrance

Hearth   Floor

extent of floor

Wall Post

0   5   10 feet

0   3 metres

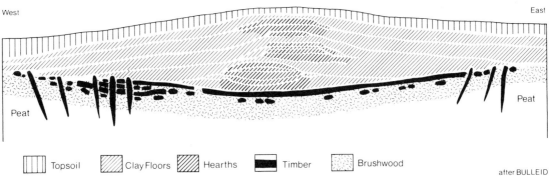

West   East

Peat   Peat

Topsoil   Clay Floors   Hearths   Timber   Brushwood

after BULLEID

39 Plan and section of Mound 74, Glastonbury Lake Village, based on Bulleid's records. This mound is representative of a group of about nine substantial structures, probably the main dwelling-houses of the village.

diameter ranged from 5.5 m to 8.5 m, but some larger spreads of clay without good evidence for walls were found, up to 12 m in diameter. The floor area of the smaller of the walled buildings described above was equivalent to that of the house in which this book is being written, which suggests that all the buildings were large enough to serve as dwellings, and the increase in size with rebuilding could reflect the growth of a household. Post-hole rings from other Iron Age sites, sometimes thought too small to represent the outer wall of a house, have diameters comparable to those from Glastonbury where we know there was a wall. Buildings 6 m across at Maiden Castle and 7 m across at Eldon's Seat (both in Dorset) fall comfortably within the 5.5–8.0 m range at Glastonbury, and at 15 m the large house from Little Woodbury (Wiltshire) is vast.

fig. 40   Bulleid suggested from the start that some of the Mounds at Glastonbury may not have had ordinary dwellings on them. One such is Mound 61, with a thick base of brushwood and timber supporting a clay floor of about 6.0 m in diameter. In the centre was a gravel hearth, and planks radiated out from this to cover most of the floor area. No evidence for walling was found nor was there any around the adjacent Mound 60. The floor and hearths of both mounds were later covered by a large spread of clay which extended over Mound 59 as well. Peas and wheat and barley were associated with the lower clay floors of Mounds 61 and 60, and in the area between them were three oak beams held down by large oak piles to make three sides of a square open to Mound 61, but apparently at the level of the substructure rather than the floor. Relatively little pottery was found, and few artifacts of any sort were directly associated with the floors, in contrast to the many and varied artifacts from Mound 62 for example. Not that Mound 62 was necessarily a dwelling, for it contained evidence for iron smelting. We shall return to the question of buildings and their functions when considering recent interpretations of the site. For the moment, let it be said that Mounds 60 and 61 may have been primarily connected with food storage and processing, and Mound 62 with ironworking, and we need not postulate a family for every floor in the village.

Bulleid also suggested that Glastonbury contained evidence for square buildings, in addition to the round ones associated with the clay floors. He stated that 'from the beginning of the exploration the writer was eagerly on the look-out for the site of a square-shaped dwelling, but no evidence of any was forthcoming.' But he did find a number of oak beams which he considered to be ground plates to hold a vertical hurdle-work wall, and under Mound 56 he found hurdle-work with sails at just the right spacing for an adjacent oak beam with a row of small mortise holes. The beams had notched ends so that they could be overlapped at right angles, and larger mortise holes at the overlap to take a corner post or stake to secure the structure. In Bulleid's view, therefore, there was good evidence for square structures, but none of it was *in situ*. He remarked that 'the rectangular dwellings were presumably of earlier date than the round, yet the workmanship of the wood and hurdles shows a more

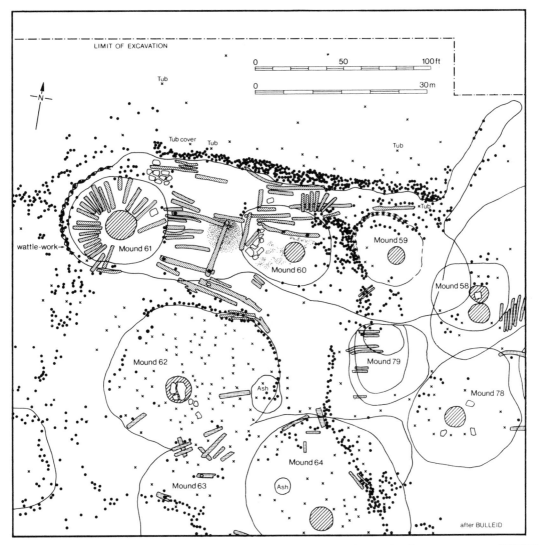

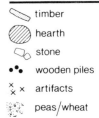

40 A northern part of Glastonbury Lake Village, based on Bulleid's plans and redrawn to show the relationship of Mounds 59–62 and 79. In the original publication, this interesting group of structures was split between four plans, making the close relationship difficult to appreciate.

advanced method and greater skill in construction than that of the round dwellings' (vol. 1, 57).

Re-interpretations of Glastonbury

Both these points – the existence of early square structures and the superiority of the earlier woodworking – were taken up by Professor E. Tratman of Bristol University. Tratman was not an archaeologist by profession, but he had long been involved with Mendip archaeology, and he was a regular visitor to the Levels. His 1970 re-interpretation of Glastonbury is based on the published site report and on Bulleid's small booklet *The Lake Villages of Somerset*, not on any firsthand acquaintance with the site. Basing his argument mainly on the site plans and on Bulleid's annotations, Tratman plotted nineteen square or *fig. 41* rectangular structures, built largely of oak, which occurred under or below the clay floors but never over them. The straight-sided structures were interpreted as houses, built on piles several feet above ground or water-level, and inhabited by people who were 'very good carpenters' and used wood extensively for everyday articles. They were not particularly interested in pottery, but made fine wooden tubs and bowls, and intricate horizontal looms, and they had lathes, wheeled vehicles, ploughs, and iron tools. He thought that the wheeled vehicles and ploughs must indicate the proximity of dryland, and postulated local tillage immediately on the south-west edge of the village, with a dryland connection to the higher land of Glastonbury. This early, square-house settlement was dated *c.* 150–60 BC, and Tratman thought that it was dismantled soon after this by people who built round, wattle houses on clay floors, made a lot of pottery, worked bone and smelted bronze, wove on vertical looms and had 'no use locally for wheeled vehicles or ploughs'. Their woodworking was much inferior to that of the earlier people. The round-house occupation was divided into four phases and Tratman suggested abandonment of the village *c.* AD 50, because of rising waters. He emphasized this last point – 'a quiet abandonment' – because there had been disagreement between Bulleid, who thought the same, and Boyd Dawkins who originally plate 72 examined the human bone from the site, and who favoured a terminal massacre.

The second re-interpretation of Glastonbury was by D. L. Clarke of Cambridge University. Clarke was not particularly interested in the abandonment of the settlement, which he attributed in passing to floods, or to growth of population beyond a manageable size. Instead, he explored at length the development and social organization of the site, the economic exploitation of the surrounding landscape and relationships with other contemporary settlements. His arguments are not easy to summarize, and the following outline concentrates on those aspects which we have found of most interest, and which have a bearing on the views of Bulleid and of Tratman.

After certain theoretical preliminaries, Clarke's paper begins with an analysis of the different 'built forms' or structures to be found within the Glastonbury settlement, and the suggestion that there were thirteen different *fig. 42* types which could be found repeatedly grouped together as 'units'. Each unit was as follows:

In one half of the unit area stands the pair of major houses (1a) one of which will have attached stables (VI) and both of which share a courtyard area (11c) and its wagon stance. In the immediate vicinity are one or two workshop huts (11b) and open work

41 *Tratman's selection from the lower timbers at Glastonbury, to show possible early phases of timber structures. One of the rectangular settings is shown enlarged at the top right.*

floors (III). In the complementary half of the unit area a minor house (1b) is linked to a subrectangular ancillary hut (byre? 11a) and nearby stands a baking hut (11d), pigsty (VII) and granary (V).

About twenty people would have lived in each unit, the minor house and its half being for female residence and activities, the major houses and their half 'familial' and multi-purpose. Using artifact distribution and Bulleid's stratigraphic observations, Clarke suggested that the settlement began as four units in the central southern part of the site, and expanded mainly northwards to reach a maximum size of seven units about a hundred years later. The population would then have been about 120 people.

Social organization was then deduced, from the distribution and the density of artifact types, and the arrangement of the different structures within a unit. The complex around Mound 42 was postulated as the wealthiest on site, a possible Headman's household, with two dependent households to the west, as these were the poorest units. Extended families lived in each unit, perhaps organized along lines similar to those described in Celtic literature or by Caesar: 'At Glastonbury, then, we have several patrilocal extended families of non-noble freemen farmers, united by kinship ties and a system of allegiance through a headman, supported by a range of dependants or clients.' These 'co-operative kin groups' achieved 'a most effective structural response to the uniquely burdensome group tasks required by their demanding but rewarding marshland home.'

Clarke then turned to the economic organization of the settlement, and its exploitation of the surrounding landscape. He drew a picture of the environment, which emphasized the contrast and probable complementarity of wetland and dryland resources, and suggested specialization and reciprocity between the marshland and the Mendip communities, focused in the case of Glastonbury on the hillfort at Maesbury. The annual cycle of farming was outlined, with 'ditched field agriculture' and winter-sown barley on an infield beside the settlement, wheat and beans spring-sown in an outfield as the winter floods receded, sheep moved between upland-winter and marshland-summer pastures, wool processed into fine embroidered cloaks and the exploitation of fish, fur and fowl from the wetlands. Clarke concluded with a model of social hierarchy in the region, with Maesbury hillfort at the apex and Glastonbury occupying but a lowly position, a hierarchy mirrored by geographical location.

This is not the place to develop a full critique of Tratman's and Clarke's reconsiderations of the Glastonbury evidence, but a few observations are irresistible. Both scholars have nudged the archaeological world into looking afresh at evidence known for so many decades that familiarity had almost come to breed contempt. In both analyses, we are invited to consider the settlement as a dynamic, changing unit adapted to a peculiar marshland environment. But the paths of development which each traces are not at all similar.

Tratman, as we have already noted, develops points originally made by Bulleid, and his drawing together of the evidence for square houses, and demonstration that some at least of these precede the round, clay floors, is perhaps the most useful aspect of his paper. He differs from Bulleid mainly in considering the structural evidence to be *in situ*, although dismantled: the square houses had been built in the marsh, and not elsewhere as Bulleid thought. Whom do we believe? Bulleid, who excavated the site, categorically stated that none of the evidence for straight-sided dwellings was *in situ*, but all

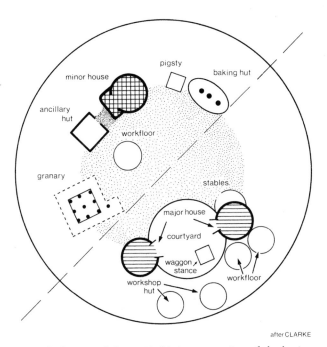

after CLARKE

42 Clarke's 'modular unit', his interpretation of the basic settlement unit at the Glastonbury Lake Village. Our own work does not support this interpretation.

was secondary, 'thrown down with other roughly shaped pieces of wood to augment the substructure under a round dwelling.' Tratman's plan, by highlighting the square-house evidence, does however show some of it to be pegged down in a regular manner, such as the two parallel beams in the area of Mounds 66, 74 and 75, or those in the area of Mounds 60, 61 and 62.

Clarke offers a third view: *in situ* square structures as Tratman suggested, but contemporary with the round structures and used as granaries or storehouses; the beams in the area between Mounds 60, 61 and 62 are given as an example. On plan the small square of these beams lies outside the clay floors, and so they could be contemporary. But, as noted above when describing Mounds 60 and 61, the beams were attributed by Bulleid to the substructure, which makes contemporaneity with the round floors unlikely. Here, it is worth quoting Bulleid's exact description, because it highlights the difficulties of deciding who, if anyone, is right. He wrote, for Mound 61 substructure:

fig. 40

In the space between this mound and Mound LX, the substructure was strengthened by mortised beams, arranged to form three sides of a square. These beams were each perforated by two mortise-holes, and were evidently in their original position, as the holes were filled by large oak piles.

These words of Bulleid's support Tratman's interpretation of square houses *in situ*, rather than his own statement that all such evidence was in a secondary position. Clarke's contemporaneity is left as possible, if not probable, since the beams are not sealed by the lower floors of Mounds 60 and 61, but only by an uppermost floor, which Bulleid notes to be continuous across Mounds 59, 60 and 61. Clarke takes account of this, attributing the granary to Phase 3 of his model, out of use by Phase 4. In this instance, it is impossible to reach a firm conclusion on the basis of the evidence available.

For the second example mentioned above – the beams between Mounds 66, 74 and 75 – there is a photograph showing one of the beams exposed 'after the removal of floor ii' of Mound 66, i.e. the lower floor of this mound, and the second beam lay 'partly under the S.E. margin of Mound LXXIV and partly under the clay of Mound LXXV.' Here, the record does not fit Clarke's interpretation of a granary or store used at a relatively late stage of the life of the settlement, and it does fit Bulleid's and Tratman's claims for square buildings preceding the clay floors. Moreover, as Bulleid states that both beams were pegged in their original positions, the honours must surely go to Tratman for advocating structures *in situ*.

Considerations of the phasing put forward by Tratman and by Clarke could easily become very tortuous, for they disagree completely in many instances although both worked from the same evidence provided by Bulleid. Table 2 sets out just a few of the differences.

TABLE 2 Glastonbury lake village phases

Mound No.	Tratman phase	Clarke phase
11	3	1
55	2	3
57	1	4
58	3	4
59	4	4
62	1	3 and 4
63	2	4
64	3	3 and 4
65	2	3 and 4
78	4	3

It will be clear that although both distinguish four phases of clay floor construction, the two systems cannot be reconciled, nor will an attempt be made here to sort out the chronology. Instead we shall turn to an aspect which Bulleid raised several times and Clarke explored at some length, namely the possibility that the settlement contained several different types of structure with different functions, rather than ninety-odd similar dwellings.

Bulleid did not venture far into the interpretation of structures, simply noting that a number of the mounds yielded too little evidence of a structural or domestic nature to be considered dwellings. Clarke, as noted above, went much further, attributing every mound and patch of clay to one of thirteen types, the types together making up his basic residential unit. Checking *fig. 42* Clarke's categories against the published evidence, some naturally fit well. For instance, his major houses more or less coincide with the mounds that had evidence for wooden floors and wattle walls, a well-marked doorway and perhaps a porch, evidence drawn together by Bulleid in his general description of the village, and used above to build up a picture of a 'typical' house. There are other structures, Clarke's minor houses, for example, which could equally well have been major houses had the model required it. But if we turn to another category, the baking huts, things do not fit so well. Clarke described the baking hut as 'an irregular clay floor with a longitudinal array of hearths and ovens covered by a light roof carried on a pair of posts – no substructure, no floorboards, no stone threshold and no porch,' and he states that 'the artifact pattern is consistent with the use of those structures as centres of female activity.' The mounds identified by Clarke as baking huts are Mounds 6, 15, 36, 37, 51 and 84. If we turn to Bulleid's descriptions of these mounds, we find a picture inconsistent with that drawn by Clarke, and no particular similarity in their features. Mound 37 did have irregular clay floors, but Mound 51 on the other hand had particularly neat circular floors. Not a single mound had 'a longitudinal array of hearths and ovens' which could have been in contemporary use; 37 is in fact the only one of these mounds to have ovens, with one hearth and one oven in possible contemporary use on three of its four floors. Mound 6 is the only one to have an 'array of hearths', but the three sets belong to successive floors and could not have been in contemporary use. Women hoping to 'gossip pleasurably in the comfort of this warm and dry micro-environment' would have been disappointed with floor iii of Mound 51 and floor i of Mound 84, neither of which had a hearth, let alone an array of them. Not one of the mounds has evidence for a pair of posts to carry the postulated light roof, although Mounds 6, 36 and 37 had a central roof post according to Bulleid. As for the lack of substructure, brushwood and sometimes timber too is recorded for all of these mounds, and 37 had a small, well-preserved platform of logs. Floorboards, stone thresholds and porches are indeed absent, but this is not particularly significant since they are absent from many another mound. The seven mounds in question are not of a special type, nor strongly associated with baking. It is not only the bakehouses which seem to be less than firmly supported by the evidence, and a much more sophisticated approach will have to be adopted to advance our understanding of the Glastonbury structures.

Bulleid's description of the setting of Glastonbury emphasized the watery surrounds, and he dug holes at some distance from the site to establish that there was a considerable depth of peat on all sides. Godwin, in 1955, described the village 'built as a raft upon the surface of a morass, supported by a multitude of piles and with open water beside it.' It comes as a surprise therefore that both Tratman and Clarke should argue for a dry, overland route to the village, and for land immediately around the site dry enough for cultivation. In addition, Clarke states that the village was built on a raised bog, a conclusion never entertained by Bulleid nor by Godwin; both are at pains to emphasize the reverse. Both Clarke and Tratman were probably misled by the complicated history of the river Brue and by the soils which formed in the vicinity of the site long after its abandonment. Godwin's stratigraphic work, and that carried out in connection with our own investigations, has shown some unexpected buried 'islands' near Westhay, but nothing of that nature near Glastonbury, and we do not think that anyone was driving chariots or wagons up to the village gate, or tilling fields just outside the palisade. Indeed, any reading of Bulleid's descriptions must surely underline the wetness of conditions beyond the palisade, which is where most of the well-preserved wooden objects were found. Clarke's winter-sown infield of barley on dryland adjacent to the village is a figment of the imagination, and Tratman's outcrops of lias clay have no better foundation.

It will be clear that we disagree with both Tratman and Clarke in a number of respects, and the disagreement is sometimes quite fundamental. However, their papers have drawn attention to aspects of the settlement too long neglected, and provoked many new thoughts concerning its *raison d'être*; to these we will return later in this chapter, bearing in mind the comment made by many scientists: a good hypothesis is worth a ton of facts.

As our own work at Glastonbury is only now underway, it is premature to set down a firm interpretive framework, but there are several obvious comments which any reading of Bulleid and Gray's texts, and our first observations on the site, will make clear. Not all of the ninety mounds were similar, and only a few held major dwelling-houses for families. Other mounds represent either general purpose or specialized areas, for the working of wood and bone, for the production of bronze and iron objects, and for the manufacture of pottery. Textiles and basketry may have been more home-based, in the actual dwellings, where baking also took place. And the function of some of these particular areas on the site will have altered through time, so a position where pottery was once made became a holding-pen for pigs or sheep, for example. We cannot say if there were clear gender differences in the use of particular structures, nor indeed if the society was male-dominated. In the absence of clear stratigraphical evidence it is probably impossible to deduce the precise phases of occupation over the 300 or 400 years of activity, although the fitting together of potsherds, for example, might provide good guides to the relationship of various tips and spreads of occupation. The settlement was

frontispiece   isolated in its watery fastness, and links by boat and raft to the nearest dryland were necessary during wet seasons, with carts and wagons made at the settlement but used primarily on the drylands where permanent fields for cultivation, woodland for coppicing, and pasture for animals, were to be found. Warlike attitudes are unlikely to have been prevalent given such a spread of activities. The palisade was probably more a breakwater than defense against attack. This very generalized picture is one capable of further refinement but only by careful statistical analysis of the spread of artifacts through reconstructed layers of occupation, as well as by an understanding of the mounding construction and post-depositional factors which can probably be obtained only through modern excavation on and around the site.

Meare

Meare, the counterpart to Glastonbury, is familiar to most people only as a second example of a wetland Iron Age settlement, and perhaps as a source of glass beads. It is rarely discussed in detail, and usually mentioned only as an afterthought to Glastonbury, reinforcing some point based on evidence from the latter. In fact, as we shall seek to demonstrate here, Meare was probably a very different site, but its contrasts to Glastonbury have been masked by the course of events relating to its excavation and publication. The site, or rather the two adjacent sites, were found by Bulleid, and he and Gray excavated them once they had completed Glastonbury. The excavations, which began in 1908, were interrupted by both World Wars, and the seasons after 1938 were conducted by Gray alone, who completed his investigations in 1956. The initial process of exploration was therefore much longer than at Glastonbury, forty-eight years as opposed to fifteen years. Gray as curator of Taunton Museum concentrated mainly on the retrieval of artifacts, and in 1956, in his early eighties, he too retired from the field.

plate 76

Meare consisted of two groups of mounds. The western half was tackled first and published in three volumes, although by 1966 when the third appeared both directors had died and it was left to Molly Cotton to edit the final volume. Bulleid and Gray's excavations in the eastern half were not published, nor have they yet been, a fact which many people do not realize since the two parts of the site are rarely distinguished in print.

fig. 43

A decade after Gray ceased excavation, Michael Avery came to investigate the site and between 1966 and 1969 he examined a number of locations at Meare East and at Meare West. A relatively full interim report on his 1966 season appeared in 1969, and the aspects of this which most people seized upon were his suggestions that the site was late Bronze Age in origin and that the clay mounds were not the remains of structures, but of rubbish dumps.

Little more happened at Meare until another decade had passed, and the Project turned to an examination of what remained, prompted in part by Clarke's analysis of Glastonbury, and in part by an awareness that what remained of the site was drying fast and little time was left for the retrieval of environmental and economic evidence, the value of which had been ignored or underestimated in earlier investigations. In 1978, we carried out preliminary work at Meare, followed by larger excavations in 1979, 1982 and 1984. At the same time, all the available data for Meare West was collected and analysed by Caroline Sturdy (now Wells) and for Meare East by Bob Silvester.

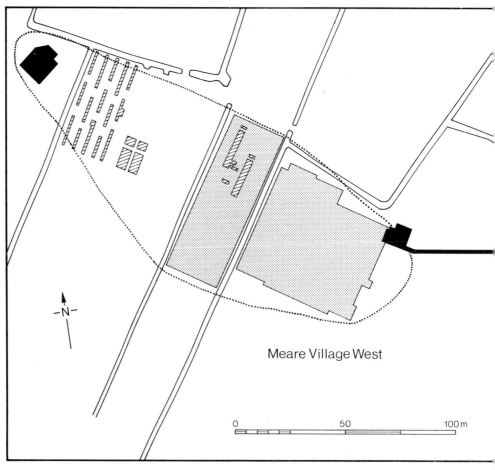

43 *Plan of the Meare Lake Villages, East and West, showing the known extent of settlement areas and all recorded excavations.*

One surprise awaited us in the field. In 1982, when we began our campaign at Meare East, we received permission to use Bulleid and Gray's old and original digging hut which had survived their work at Glastonbury, Meare West and Meare East, over a period of sixty years, and which now stood abandoned and boarded-up on a mound at Meare East. We broke in, to find not only a dry and entirely usable hut, but a box of Iron Age pottery from one of the last seasons of Gray's excavations (1955), some animal bone and heaps of pebbles and broken querns, all presumably abandoned as unimportant or too heavy to move at the end of his final season. The hut had three rooms, a central work-room, and two offices (one at each side) in which Bulleid and Gray had their allotted places. In Gray's office, behind his work top, lay a heap of old newspapers, apparently the residue of daily readings; they covered some of the years from 1956 back to 1890, spanning the whole episode at

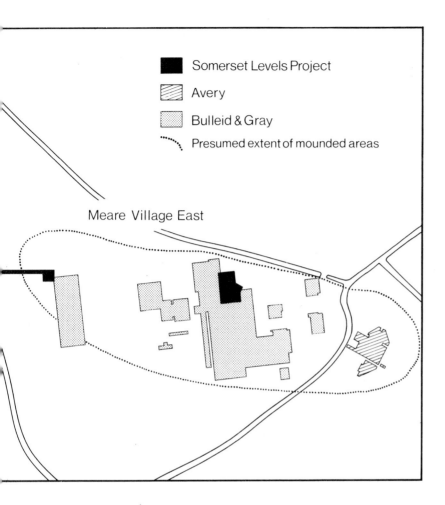

Glastonbury and Meare. In the early years, he read *The Times*; by the 1930s he was a *Daily Telegraph* reader.

Our excavations of 1978, 1979 and 1982 are published, and thanks to the encouragement and assistance of the Historic Buildings and Monuments Commission, moves are now once more under way to publish the earlier excavations of Bulleid and Gray at Meare East and Avery's subsequent work. This history of work at Meare may seem lengthy to the reader, yet it is but a brief outline of a complex sequence of events which reflects not only the vagaries of a particular site but also much of the course of British archaeology in this century. It shows only too well how excavation is destruction, and total destruction if the results are not published.

Let us turn now from what we do not know about Meare to what we do know. The two groups of mounds were situated just off the northern edge of

Meare island. Godwin has demonstrated that they were on the edge of a raised bog, which flourished to the north and west. To the east, conditions were wetter, a sea of rush and sedge, but not the open-water marsh that surrounded Glastonbury. Nor was Meare surrounded by a palisade, perhaps because there was less need for a foundation and so no demand for a retaining wall. Otherwise, the spreads of mounds were similar to those observed at Glastonbury: superimposed clay floors with hearths that tended to be renewed more often than the floors, and scattered settlement debris of pottery, bone, cereal and beans and a host of other artifacts. The settlement at Meare started as occupation on the raised bog surface, without any clay floors, but as conditions deteriorated, clay was imported to keep out the damp. Few traces of superstructure indicate that the Meare buildings were relatively flimsy, perhaps tents, as suggested by Bulleid and reiterated by the present authors in recent years. Despite this, Meare has yielded an abundance of evidence for artifact manufacture and artifact use, for the bone refuse of slaughtered animals and for plant foods; it was not an impoverished site.

This much was clear from an early stage of our work and one of the challenges facing us was to discover why a settlement in such an apparently damp and barren location should have flourished, as Meare did for several centuries in the later Iron Age. On the one hand, our programmes of sieving and analyses of pollen and plant macrofossil remains, of beetles and of animal bones, had confirmed and filled out the picture of a flourishing economic base. On the other hand, the same plant and beetle analyses had demonstrated a degree of wetness inimical to year-round occupation of the site. We concluded that Meare had been a seasonal settlement.

We were sure, and remain sure, that Meare itself was the site of a settlement and not simply the recipient of debris from a dryland site. But the impoverished setting, in ecological terms, remained at odds with the wealth of food debris and with the artifact evidence that accumulated from our excavations and from the data retrieved from earlier sites. We found, for example, that even the minor occupation at the extreme west of Meare West,

plate 77
plate XVI

examined in 1979, yielded an extraordinarily varied range of manufactured goods: iron and bronze, tin and lead, glass, wood, pots, loom-weights, bone and antler, all within a relatively small area. Moreover, there was strong evidence for the local manufacture of some of these articles, including part-worked bone, bronze drips and crucible fragments. Most significantly, Julian Henderson of Bradford University demonstrated that glass had been worked into beads on the site, thus providing the first positive identification of a glass bead manufactory from the southern British Iron Age. A summer settlement, rich in food and possessions, bringing in raw materials and turning them into fine objects, some of which, like the glass beads, were to reach other sites in due course, seemed to us to be no farming hamlet. And who would farm on a raised bog? Neither sheep nor wheat like acid wetness. Instead, we consider Meare as the site of an annual trade fair where people from far and wide, and perhaps from the three adjacent tribal territories of the Dobunni, Durotriges and Dumnonii, met on neutral ground to feast and to make and exchange their wares.

When the early excavations of Meare are fully published, and our own analyses completed, this picture may be modified. However much it alters, some similarities and contrasts with Glastonbury will hold firm. Meare was built with clay floors laid directly on a raised bog surface. At Glastonbury, there was no stable surface, only a 'morass', to use Godwin's evocative term, and a foundation of timber and brushwood was required. So Glastonbury was a crannog and Meare was not. Glastonbury yielded good structural evidence and much well-preserved worked wood, Meare did not. The difference probably stems from the initial differences in the degree of wetness, in so far as wooden artifacts are concerned, because at Glastonbury discarded artifacts sank into the soft peat outside the palisade whereas at Meare they could only moulder on the raised bog surface and many would have been washed away in the winter floods. The lack of structural evidence at Meare, compared with Glastonbury, could be due to the slightly drier conditions at Meare causing wattle walls to rot away, but the base of posts of round houses should have survived, and only a few did; burnt daub, which was often found at Glastonbury, should have survived equally well at Meare had it ever been present, but little was found. Therefore, we remain inclined to agree with Bulleid that the people at Meare were sheltered under lighter, less permanent superstructures than at Glastonbury.

Artifacts from the settlements

Before we speculate further on the nature of the two sites, let us glance at the artifacts which were recovered from them. Because of the wet conditions, bone was very well-preserved, and because the sites were protected by overlying deposits, and never ploughed or otherwise seriously disturbed, artifacts of all types have survived in a much better state than is the norm on dryland sites. The pottery from Glastonbury and Meare is well-known for its fine decoration and for the analyses of the different fabrics used in its manufacture, carried out by David Peacock. By studying the plain ware as well as the decorated, Sue Rouillard has identified a wide range of fabrics, and found that the same fabric might be used to make both plain and decorated pots, perhaps of identical shape. Occasionally, pots of almost identical shape and decoration have been identified from Meare West and Meare East, and also from Glastonbury, suggesting close links between the sites. There is also similarity in the style of decoration on pots and that found on some of the wooden tubs from Glastonbury.

These tubs are precisely the sort of objects which were in common use on prehistoric settlements, just as they were on medieval and later settlements until the Industrial Revolution brought cheap metal dishes and pans and, later,

plates xv–xvi

fig. 44

fig. 45 plastics. Around Glastonbury, remains of fourteen tubs or smaller containers were found, some hollowed out of a solid piece of wood and others made of staves which were either dowelled together, or held by hoops like a barrel. One small tub, hollowed out of a block of ash, was 15 cm high and about 30 cm in diameter with sides and base 2 cm thick or less, and it may originally have had a handle. A delicate curvilinear pattern had been incised and burned on the outer surface, and this was obviously a container of some beauty, to be classed amongst fine wooden bowls rather than as a lowly kitchen tub. Another well-finished wooden container was a little stave-built tub of oak, with four legs formed by a continuation of staves below the inserted base. Its height, including the legs, was just over 15 cm and it was nearly 25 cm in diameter. The staves were dowelled together with little oak pegs, and held by a bronze band around their middle. These two tubs, and the several others where enough has survived for a conjectural reconstruction, are shown in fig. 45, as they might originally have looked.

44 *Reconstruction drawing of pottery from Glastonbury and Meare.*

45 *Reconstruction drawing of basketry and wooden tubs and bowls, based on Bulleid's records for Glastonbury and Meare.*

Basketry was used for larger containers, fragments of which survived both at Glastonbury and at Meare. One was plain but neatly made with single ribs up to 12 mm in diameter and interwoven withies 3–6 mm in diameter. Another had double or triple ribs and the suggestion of a patterned weave, and the basketry from Meare was patterned. The original size of these lightweight containers is not known, but they may have been at least 60–90 cm high and the same across, laundry basket rather than waste-paper basket in their capacity.

We suspect that leather containers were also in use, of the goatskin water bag or leather winebottle variety. The reason for this is that several wooden bungs or stoppers were found, but nothing to put them in. Had they stopped up pottery casks or wooden tubs, both container and stopper should have survived in the peat, but had the container been leather and the stopper wood, no trace of the bag would have been left in the peat. The stoppers were made of oak, about 7 cm long and 3–5 cm at their maximum diameter.

fig. 46

The inventory of wooden household objects continues with ladles. Their bowls were from 7–10 cm across, and the handle of one complete specimen was 12 cm long, with a knob at the end. Various other wooden pegs and pounder-like pieces may have had a household function, but we cannot determine exactly what this was.

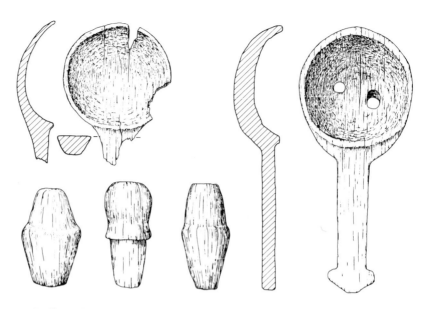

46 *Ladles and stoppers from Glastonbury. The short-handled ladles were probably used in cooking or eating, and the stoppers may have been for leather bags. Scale 1:3.*

Wood was also used for the handles of knives, and a host of other iron tools. On the whole, the wooden handles are better preserved than the iron blades, but sufficient remains of the latter to gain an impression of the complete original object and its function. It is surprising how familiar many of the forms appear, with axes and adzes, billhooks, sickles, saws and files and knives of various sizes. The billhooks had a curved iron blade 20–30 cm long, and a straight, wooden handle about twice as long as the blade. A narrow saw blade, just over 20 cm long, had a very fine, curved, ash handle ending in a knob, and sickles or reaping hooks also had knobbed handles. Either oak or ash were used to make these handles, although the adze handles seem to have been exclusively of ash, and the only gouge handles identified were of oak. Perhaps an adze, swung at a heavy timber, needed a resilient, springy handle, whereas a gouge, held firm and hammered with a mallet, needed a different sort of strength. What the mallets were like is also known, thanks to the wet peat which preserved two examples at Glastonbury, and their form is very similar to that of a modern one. The cylindrical head, 15–17 cm long and 7–10 cm in diameter, had flat or slightly convex ends, and was pierced by a hole which took the wooden handle. One handle 28 cm long has survived. The wood used for these mallets was not identified, but we may assume that it was not oak or ash since Bulleid would have recognized these. It might have been yew, as in the case of the Neolithic mallet found on Meare Heath.

plate 79

As with the household items, many other objects were recovered which were probably used as tools around the house and farmyard, but their function is no longer clear. Foremost amongst these are Bulleid's 'sixty-three pieces of framework, presumably parts of looms or appliances for making textile fabric'. They were mostly made from ash, with some oak, and they had a variety of mortise holes and tenons which showed that they were meant to fit together to make a rectangular frame, apparently about 80 × 50 cm in one case. This is not very large, certainly not on the scale of contemporary vertical weaving looms, and the small holes down the edges of the frame suggest that something was stretched, in two directions, inside. They are not appropriate for threading warp. Clarke suggested that they were embroidery frames, or frames for drying small animal pelts, and to these possibilities we would add chariot or cot panels.

plate 78

Evidence for weaving is nevertheless plentiful from both sites. Sheep are the most common domestic animal, and many died old enough to have provided their owners with several fleeces. Spindle-whorls indicate that the wool was spun locally, and the diversity of materials used to make these little items, and the decoration on some of them, suggests that spinning was a public and pleasurable occupation. Some were made of clay, many of stone of different sorts, and bone and antler were occasionally used. Ammonites with a hole pierced through their centre may have been spindle-whorls, and perhaps the most unusual example, to our minds, was a disc of human skull bone, just about the right size to have served as a whorl.

Loom-weights of clay indicate that the spun wool was woven into cloth on the settlement, on vertical looms which were probably supported by two upright posts, but no exact location for a loom has yet been identified. It is a great pity that no cloth has been found either, because the skills shown in the production of other materials, the use of colour evident in glass and enamel work, the sense of pattern displayed in decorating wood and pottery, suggest that it might have been very fine. But wool, like leather, is of animal origin and decays in the peat.

Here we should also mention the many antler combs from the settlements. These were originally described as weaving combs, and thought to be used to push up the weft on the loom. Experimental work has indicated that the combs would not function very well as weaving accessories, but they might perhaps have been used at an earlier stage of wool production, to clean the fleeces. They could also have served to remove hair from skins prior to tanning. Several hundred of the combs were found at Meare, and it may be that they were used both industrially and as personal equipment.

plate XV

Personal ornaments are well represented at both sites. As many of these are the sort of objects which are well known elsewhere, brooches and bracelets and rings from burials for example, we will concentrate here on the glass beads. Glastonbury and Meare have proved rich sources of coloured glass bead, some plain yellow or blue or bluish green and others decorated with

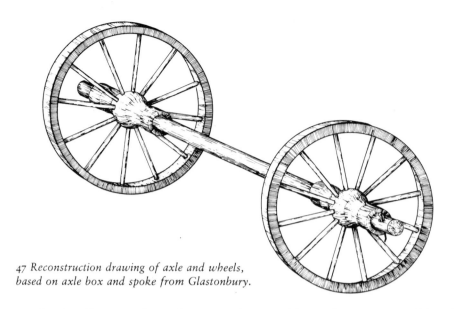

47 *Reconstruction drawing of axle and wheels,*
based on axle box and spoke from Glastonbury.

swirls of yellow on clear glass, or white on blue. The quantity of beads, especially from Meare, was such that the settlements were often suggested as centres of production, and Gray thought the evidence from Glastonbury pointed to manufacture there. But it was not until 1979 that evidence was uncovered at Meare West to prove that beads were made on the spot. The evidence came from beads that went wrong and were thrown away. One was made of blue glass, wound around a metal rod, and another was of multi-coloured glass encased in a mould. Bulleid and Gray recovered possible necklaces of beads from Meare East, and single specimens have been found scattered elsewhere, so it is likely that people were wearing as well as making these colourful ornaments.

If Meare was the site of an annual fair, we must assume that people and goods were travelling in from the settlements around. Some would have walked, but at Glastonbury evidence was found for a dugout canoe, and other dugouts are known from the region. That watercraft were in use is not at all surprising, given the local environment, and the Glastonbury canoe, at least 6.5 m long, could have carried several people and their goods through the reedy waters to the vicinity of Meare. Wheeled vehicles were in use for dryland transport, either two-wheeled carts or four-wheeled wagons. Those equipped with solid oak wheels must have lumbered along, whilst lighter vehicles with *fig. 47* spoked wheels sped by. Details of the latter wheels are clear from the Glastonbury evidence, where one axle box, for example, was made to hold an axle 8 cm in diameter and twelve spokes 3 cm in diameter. A nearby spoke was nearly 30 cm long, and put together, the wheel would have been 80 cm in diameter, allowing for an outer, wooden felly and iron tyre such as those known from the Yorkshire cart burials of Iron Age date. This is a good deal larger than a modern bicycle wheel.

Many items of harness indicate that horses were used for transport, either to pull vehicles or to carry a rider. Iron bits were found, and bronze terret rings, and antler cheek-pieces, as well as various items that may have decorated a leather harness. It is generally assumed that horses pulled the lighter vehicles, perhaps a two-wheeled cart or chariot, whilst oxen dragged the heavier solid-wheeled wagons. The bones of both animals have been found, the remains of horses indicating a slender animal of about 11 to 12 hands or sometimes slightly larger, but never more than pony-sized. The cattle were also small, a few inches shorter at the shoulder than the ponies.

Interpretation

Many artifacts were made within the settlements of Glastonbury and Meare, and at Meare in particular the debris of craft and industrial production abounds. We have already commented on spinning and weaving, and glass-bead production. To these we should add the working of bone and antler, to make the weaving combs for example, or toggles and needles and counters. Shale was turned into bracelets, probably using a lathe, and it seems likely that lathes were used in the production of some of the wooden tubs and wheels. Much other woodworking took place within the villages to make objects of everyday use, together with that required for building the Glastonbury foundations, palisade and houses. Perhaps most surprising, given the location of the sites at some distance from metal ores, both bronze and iron were apparently smelted, and bronze at least was cast, and it seems that some of the smithing was carried out within the houses at Glastonbury, perhaps rather unwisely. Mounds 5 and 62 provided evidence for tuyères, small furnaces, and crucibles. The floor of Mound 62, where the smithing evidence was found, was covered with burnt daub, ash and charcoal, and the tops of the wall posts were charred. It is tempting to suggest that the smithing set fire to the building.

plate XVI

The occupation of the two sites is not very well dated, despite the numbers of diagnostic artifacts and the recent application of radiocarbon assay and dendrochronology. The problems derive mainly from the very uncertain stratigraphy of the sites, and the lack of context for many of the artifacts. This is not only due to the way Bulleid and Gray recorded their excavation, but also to the original nature of the deposits in and around the settlements, with few firm surfaces where a discarded object would come to rest, conveniently in association with its contemporaries and duly sealed by later deposits. Instead, rubbish was swirled around by floodwaters, picked up and redeposited in a new context, or left to sink through the softer peats to a level well below the surface contemporary with its use. At Meare, we were able to demonstrate the mixing of material as deposits were formed, by joining potsherds from different layers. At Glastonbury, conditions were softer, and the mixing was probably even greater. Nevertheless, we do regret the lack of context for objects found under, in and above the clay floors of the mounds, because much could have been learnt from such information about the way the floors were built up and about their subsequent collapse. Lacking this evidence, it is hard to 'phase' the site, and the almost total disagreement of Tratman and Clarke on phasing is symptomatic of the problems. It is possibly also a reflection of their individual enthusiasms to obtain more from the evidence than the evidence was capable of yielding. The site was and is exceptional, but the conditions of environment and excavation militate against the 'perfect preservation' view.

To return to dates (and here we are for once dealing with dates in calendar years), Bulleid and Gray placed the foundation of Meare at about 250 BC, and its end 'well into the Roman period' and they held that Glastonbury was founded later and abandoned sooner, before the Roman Conquest. Tratman placed the beginning of his square-house phase at Glastonbury at about 150 BC, the beginning of the clay-floor phase at about 50 BC and final abandonment at about AD 50. Clarke placed Glastonbury between 150 ± 50 and 50 ± 50 BC. In the interim report on his excavations at Meare, Avery discusses the phasing and dates of the settlement and suggests the first Iron Age occupation was in the third century BC, continuing into the second century BC, whereafter people lived nearby but not actually out on the raised bog, until some slight re-occupation in the third or fourth century AD. Our excavations at Meare in 1979 produced samples of wood and peat for radiocarbon assay, and these together with Ruth Morgan's tree-ring work suggested occupation from the third century BC. Evidence found at Meare East in 1982 pointed to later occupation at that particular spot, in that artifacts of late first century BC and first century AD were found, and sherds of Iron Age, Roman and Medieval date were found lying virtually side by side on a mound surface. Bulleid and Gray's original estimate for the date and duration of occupation at Meare therefore holds good in the light of recent evidence, but our understanding of the sequence of development at either site has not been greatly advanced. Dendrochronology is the one sure way of refining the chronology of the sites, but for that we need wood, and there is little left to be analysed from either site.

We may conclude this survey of the two wetland settlements with a brief consideration of their role in the regional community. Clarke put Glastonbury firmly in the territory of the late Iron Age tribe of the Dumnonii, whereas Cunliffe has more recently drawn the border between the Durotriges and the Dobunni roughly east-west through Meare Pool, with the Dumnonii well distant. In actual fact, the links and affinities shown in the material culture of the two sites are far-flung, whether one looks at pottery fabrics and pot styles, which suggest contacts to the south and south-west, or the origins of quern-stones which are to the north and north-east, or coins and currency bars, or, considering exports, the eventual distribution of the beads which were produced at Meare. Neither site was isolated, nor were contacts solely in one direction. We do not, for example, accept Clarke's Glastonbury–Maesbury axis as having any greater strength than the links with other contemporary groups in the region, and there were plenty of these, from the cave-dwellers of Wookey Hole in the Mendips to the occupants of small hillforts on Maesbury and Dundon, or of major fortified sites at South Cadbury and Ham Hill. Some of the islands in the Levels, such as Westonzoyland and Alstone, were settled in this period, and Brent Knoll, surrounded perhaps at times by the sea, was another contemporary site.

The scene is one of varied settlement types, specializing in order to exploit different ecological niches as the landscape filled up with an expanding late Iron Age population. In this context, we see Glastonbury and Meare as adaptations to the wetland niche. Meare exploited the marginal qualities of the raised bog, in that a particularly impoverished environment was selected as the meeting-place for people from all around the region, and perhaps from three different tribes. In such a spot, no one was going to flare up in anger because the sheep had broken into his wheat, or the cattle were eating the coppice, or children were scaring off the wild game. The setting was ideal for lowering the potential tensions of a large gathering, and for offering space for families of farmers and craftsmen and their stock so that they need not tread on one another's toes. At Glastonbury, people may have been farmers, but with fields on the islands of Godney or Meare, not in the marsh. They had better sense than to attempt to drain the latter, *pace* Clarke's ditched field agriculture; instead, they specialized in exploiting the resources of the shallow lake, especially the birds (whose presence introduced this chapter) and fish, and perhaps the furry otter and beaver. Maybe they also exploited the marsh as a place of refuge, a hidden stronghold: the prehistoric equivalent of King Alfred's Sedgemoor retreat of Aethelney.

8 Draining the future

al the plaine marsche ground at sodaine raynes wold be
overflowen, and the profite of the meade lost

(Leland)

To the traveller hastening his way to the south-west, the uncompromisingly
flat landscape of the Levels may seem dreary and discouraging. Yet it does not
take long for anyone working in the Levels to comprehend and absorb the
beauty and fascination of the wetland, and for us the experience of over fifteen
years has not stilled the imagination or exhausted the enthusiasm for the vast
expanses of bright meadow and rhyne, mottled woodland or dark peatfield. In
this book we have been unable to devote much space to the natural beauty of
the landscape, but working amidst the myriad of flowering plants and
abundant wildlife is a constant if ever-changing reminder of the immediacy of
contact between environment and man. Perhaps in no other than a wetland
landscape is the relationship so apparent.

Wetland as an archaeological landscape has only recently been recognized
as a unique and threatened archaeological resource, and few textbooks refer to
wetlands as a specific environment requiring special treatment. As our work
developed over the years, a number of wetland characteristics were identified,
and we think it will be useful to list them here as indicators of why we were
attracted to Somerset in the first place, and why we persisted in the work. They
will also serve to illustrate the contribution of the Levels to the developing
science of wetland archaeology.

1.   Wetlands can provide unexpected kinds of evidence, discoveries of
artifacts and other types of information that are totally unrepresented on
dryland sites. The Neolithic God-Dolly from the Bell track is an excellent
example of this, as nothing in the previous archaeological record of Britain
gave any hint of the existence of such a peculiar object. Perhaps more
predictable but nonetheless unusual is the two-pronged fork from Skinner's
Wood, a tool of immense practical value in the reed and sedge beds of the
Bronze Age.

2.   A second wetland advantage is best described in terms of the totality of
evidence on sites. Because waterlogging inhibits decay, many more objects will
survive 'time's arrow' in a complete state, and among these the wooden bows
and the yew mallet, from Neolithic peats on Meare Heath, are just those

plate VII

plate 59

fig. 23
plate 38

184

artifacts we presume Neolithic people made and used, but for which we have nothing from dry sites but circumstantial evidence, basically flint arrowheads and post-holes. In the same way, the preservative qualities of the peats around the Sweet Track have guaranteed the immaculate survival of flint tools, so that their handling and the materials on which they were used can be identified.

fig. 14

plate 80

3.   This totality, or near-totality, of material culture is not restricted to mere survival. Because many wetlands are regularly inundated by water, the materials of ancient man are not left exposed to the destructive elements of air, heat, erosion and scavenging animals, including man. Many observations of recent communities, and common sense, show that an abandoned site is soon cleared of its valuable and usable materials, from small dropped artifacts to parts of structures. In a wetland site, deserted because of the onset of flooding, deposition of clay or formation of peat, such scavenging is less likely if not impossible. Thus any real wetland site acquires its 'totality of evidence' by the inhibition of natural decay and the discouragement of scavenging. The enormous wealth and variety of artifacts from the Iron Age settlement of Glastonbury reflects these inhibitions.

plate XVI

4.   Although some wetland sites represent occupations over long periods of time, the progressive build-up of deposits should be identifiable through good stratigraphical control in excavation, though in fact at Meare we can demonstrate animal disturbance and floodwater erosion. Other sites will have been overwhelmed by water, peat or clay so rapidly that they can be shown to be single-event, short-lived occupations or activities. As such, they provide us with an all-too-rare look at a prehistoric event, one that is not masked by incorporation in previous and subsequent events of the past, or mis-identified by archaeological digging. The planning, construction and use of the Sweet Track, for example, occupied a Neolithic community for less than a single generation; a Neolithic child born in the year of its construction was still a child when it was abandoned and lost for 6000 years.

plate 24

5.   Wetlands are, of course, unique in their daily, seasonal or ultimate inundation. They submerge and preserve an episode or episodes of wetland conditions so rapidly that their contemporary environments can be analysed with a precision far surpassing that of dry landscapes where erosion and leaching can occur. The reconstruction of dryland environments through pollen analysis is often important for the regional picture, and soil and molluscan analyses can often define the conditions more precisely. But a wetland peatbog, for example, where pollen, fungi, leaves and twigs, beetles and other insects and spiders will be preserved, can provide quite exceptional definition to environmental studies. The Sweet Track again is a good example of this precision.

plate 22

6.   In terms of ancient economies, the wetland record is not as uniformly good. Many wetlands, including peatbogs, are harsh on some materials and bone is a notable example of rapid degradation in an acidic environment. Yet such conditions are not always present, and the prolific bone industry and

plate XV midden deposits at Meare, allied to the good preservation of seeds and other plant remains, show the potential yield of information about ancient economies that some wetland sites afford.

7.   It may seem unneccessary to comment further on the preservative qualities of wetlands, but there is a negative aspect. Most wetlands will preserve wood, and therefore its absence will be significant in particular circumstances. An axe on a dryland site is generally presumed to have had a wooden haft decayed to plate 29 oblivion; an axe in a peatbog should have its haft preserved. The purpose of the unhafted jadeite axe from the Sweet Track may not be understood, but plate VIII track-building was not among its uses.

In sum, a wetland environment will often create or encourage conditions which allow extremely good preservation of a wide range of materials, held in place and rapidly sealed. By careful recovery and analysis of this surviving evidence, in its context and its contemporary environments, we are offered unique opportunities for reconstructing patterns of settlement and behaviour, and for comprehending the processes at work in the development of those social, economic, perhaps political, even sometimes ideological, factors which went to form the ancient societies which we study. There are no better environments for such work.

Evidence at risk

Over the past twenty years, our work in the Somerset Levels has succeeded, we think, in establishing the nature and extent of human interest in the area over a period of about 4000 years. We have missed much, through unobserved peat-cutting, and more finds almost certainly lie hidden beneath the grassland pastures in the northern Brue valley and on Sedgemoor. It is this buried evidence that is now at risk through the relentless drainage and progressive dewatering of the wetlands. But no area in the world which was once inhabited by man has retained a complete record of that presence, and archaeology as a science has to accept that it works with a fragmentary record, and devise ways to augment it by ever more disciplined and imaginative approaches to the evidence. Those discoveries which have enormously increased our information include the drowned Neolithic and Bronze Age settlements of the European Alpine lakes, the peat-buried trackways and bog-bodies of northern Germany and southern Denmark, and the burial platforms and settlements in the sloughs and swamps of Florida and in the mud-slides and middens of the Pacific Coast of North America. To the increasingly rich yield of information from these regions, we think the Somerset Levels make a contribution and a unique one, essentially as an environmentally precise and culturally organic wetland. The absence of some types of evidence from the Levels is countered in part by the excellent preservation of other aspects, particularly wood.

It will be clear that our evidence is not like that from a normal dryland

British site, where flint, stone, pottery and post-holes assume such importance. Our evidence is different, and we think it is unusual enough to warrant efforts on two fronts. One, the visible work of excavation and publication allows our evidence to stand beside that recovered from dryland sites, each complementing the other to increase our knowledge of British prehistory. Just as dryland evidence does not give the whole picture of what happened in the past, neither does wetland evidence alone; both must be used, to provide that totality of landscape and activities on and in which ancient man was engaged.

The second effort required is of wider concern, as it involves not only those interested in past human activities, but also all those who have a concern for the preservation of our heritage. Theodore Roosevelt, politician and conservationist, said early in this century: 'The nation behaves well if it treats the natural resources as assets, which it must turn over to the next generation increased and not impaired in value.' Would that our present politicians were as enlightened. The current developments which we can observe in the Levels do not give much cause for satisfaction or complacency. Peat-cutting as a home-based industry has existed for centuries, and was accepted as one of the mainstays of human existence in the watery landscapes of the Levels. The recent increases in peat extraction rates, with machine-cutting, are only a logical and modern development of this, and have led to hundreds of archaeological discoveries. But in doing so, peat-cutting destroys part and sometimes all of the ancient structures, and without a consistent archaeological presence our records would be a tiny fraction of what we have today. We have referred already to the loss of evidence concerning the activities of the first millennia BC and AD, through medieval and later cutting of the uppermost peats around the many hamlets of the Brue valley. The pros and cons of peat-cutting are well illustrated by Sedgemoor, where there has been no peat-cutting and where our archaeological knowledge is minimal compared to that for the Brue valley.

Less visibly destructive is drainage, often a part of the peat-cutting operation but increasingly used to further the aims of the farming industry, for which the Somerset Levels are justly famous. The history of land-drainage is long and varied. Medieval reclamation involved the digging of new rhynes to help the water to drain away, and to ensure a slightly longer growing season for crops or grass. The wettest peats of the Brue were generally avoided in this small-scale work as the area was acidic, sterile and poor in plant nutrients, as well as uncontrollably flooded because of its low altitude and lack of natural drainage. The Brue valley was only drained naturally by the river of that name, flowing past Glastonbury, through Godney island and northwards to the Bleadney Gap where the outliers of the Mendip Hills allowed the river access into the valley of the Axe. This river flow, now marked by field patterns and meandering rhyne lines, was effective only for the extreme eastern part of the whole region, and left the great raised bogs to the west more or less as a self-contained unit, hindered from a westward drainage by the flood clays of the coastal belt which overrode the edges of the original raised bog, as Godwin has so clearly demonstrated.

In the thirteenth century, if not before, the Abbots of Glastonbury had realigned both the Brue and its tributaries from the east, the rivers Sheppey and Hartlake, in order to direct them into the Meare Pool. This drained some land near Glastonbury for cultivation, and the old and new channels continued to operate for several centuries. The effect was to greatly increase the size of Meare Pool, as well as to diminish the flow of water to the Axe.

Mere-pool, as it was formerly known, has probably existed for at least 3000 years in varying guises, sometimes large and sometimes small, but always forming a kind of sump for the waters of Brue, southern slopes of the Wedmore ridge, and various other streams and outflows from the great raised bogs around it. According to Glastonbury legends, Mere-pool was instantaneously formed by the prayers of Saint Benignus to create a fishery reserved exclusively for the Abbot of Glastonbury's use; this is probably a fishy story of somewhat gigantic proportions.

plate 6

The draining of Meare Pool was a longer episode. The pool was described in 1535 as 'a fysshyng . . . whiche ys in circuite fyve myles and one myle and an half brode, wherein are greate abundance of pykes, tenchards, roches and yeles, and of dyvers other kyndes of fysshes . . . and . . . a game of swannes . . . and . . . certayne heronsewes', and by Leland two years later as a pool 'at high waters in winter a 4 miles in cumpace, and when it is lest a 2 miles and an half and most communely 3 miles'. By the year 1630, William Freake 'had drayned manie hundred acres of ground there', and most of the land thus reclaimed was turned to meadow. There still remained much open water, which is depicted on maps of 1610, 1695, 1723 and 1736, but not 1741 or later; the final act of drainage was accomplished by clearing and extending channels to link with the Brue, now flowing westwards along the line previously made by the Glastonbury estates, probably in the twelfth to thirteenth centuries. Although the Pool was often flooded in winter after 1741, it was effectively now a drained area which could be counted as a landholding, and no longer measured in terms of fish and eel yields.

The effects of drainage on the moors, as well as on the Pool, were dramatic, and not only for the peatland itself. Any extension of commonable peat wastes, i.e. land that was dry enough for long enough to provide grazing, 'enabled the poor man to support his family and bring up his children. Here he could turn out his cow and pony, feed his flock of sheep and keep his pig.' The

plate 1

problem was that winter flooding still occurred, and the commoners had no other land to use, so their cattle often starved; it was only with the passage of time, and increased drainage, that the pattern became successful. Yet not everyone was satisfied, particularly the church, as a 1798 complaint records:

the possession of a cow or two, with a hog, and a few geese, naturally exalts the peasant, in his own conception, above his brethren in the same ranks of society. It inspires some degree of confidence in a property, inadequate to his support. In sauntering after his cattle, he acquires a habit of indolence. Quarter, half and occasionally whole days are imperceptibly lost. Day-labour becomes disgusting; the aversion increases by indulgence; and at length the sale of a half-fed cow, or hog, furnishes the means of adding intemperance to idleness.

However, all was not lost, and by 1853 it could be recorded that through drainage of the moors, the cottagers who had been famous for their 'idleness, poverty and a species of sheep-stealing that evaded the existing laws made against it' had now combined into 'reputable villages'.

Today, by major works of channelling, barrages and tidal sluices, the influence of tides can be restrained, the potential floodwaters contained and diverted, and pumping established to break the hold on the Levels that the water formerly possessed unhindered. We can see the effects of such massive works on the Levels not only in the desiccation of the peat and its content, but also in the alteration of the traditional ways of life of the inhabitants. Dairy farming, with its seasonal pattern of land use, is now in the process of transition to more intensive methods of food production, including arable cultivation for vegetables, fruit and cereals. The effects of permanent drainage operations are not confined to farming of course, and there are profound changes in wildlife, including the disappearance of certain species of plant and animal.

For archaeology, drainage means the irreversible decay of the organic evidence of the past, for so long held in waterlogged peat. Fragile remains disintegrate first, the soft-bodied spiders, leaves and fibres, then wood itself dries and is attacked by organisms, seeds distort, and rapidly the archaeological remains become unworthy of retrieval, granted the pressing needs that exist elsewhere in the wetlands. Given the pace of man's insatiable demand for subsistence-productive land, there seems little hope of reversing the trend. However, there has been a notable revival of interest in the wetlands of Britain, and active steps have been taken by many agencies and parties to invest in the preservation of parts of the Somerset Levels. The Nature Conservancy Council, a variety of wildlife interests, and the County Council itself are making efforts to protect various areas of the Levels where wildlife may survive in its watery environment.

Protecting the past

Our archaeological purpose in the Levels has been defined as the identification of sites of importance, the preservation of such sites if possible, and their excavation if preservation is not feasible. In order to comply with these aims, and to react to the many threats to the environment, we have tried to work with all interests in the Levels, both the 'developers' and the 'protectors'. With the aid of peat companies and farmers, close watch of their work has resulted in multitudes of finds, to be investigated in advance of damage or destruction. With the aid of the conservation interests, various areas have been identified as exceptional, and here we have had some success in their protection.

In our work along the Sweet Track on Shapwick Heath, we identified an area where the track lay buried within a Nature Reserve. This Reserve, owned by the Eclipse Peat Works and leased to the Nature Conservancy Council, was under threat through drainage of water around the edges, and it lay within a peat-cutting area. The Somerset Levels Project had already shown the national importance of the Sweet Track through its investigations both south and north of the Reserve, and we carried out a series of small examinations of the track in the Reserve, and in fact over its entire length, to test degrees of waterlogging and general conditions. With this assessment, we could set out our priorities for preservation, and the whole 500 m of track in the Nature Reserve seemed

fig. 9 worthy of protection. Negotiations in 1983 between the Department of the Environment and the Nature Conservancy Council enabled the latter to obtain a large grant from the National Heritage Fund to purchase the Reserve from the Eclipse Peat Works (Fisons plc) at a price well below the going-rate for good quality peatland. The area was then scheduled as an Ancient Monument, and so protected from future peat extraction or any destructive work. Arrangements were made for the building of a clay bank around part of the Reserve, and long-term agreements reached for the pumping-in of water during dry seasons to keep the peat and the track wet. Tubes have been sunk along the line of the track to monitor the water-levels. The Sweet Track therefore appears to be safe here from peat-cutting, from archaeologists, and from desiccation, and in the face of the formidable problems confronting this particular wetland, we think the solution is admirable, so long as water supplies remain at hand.

Of the many other structures buried in the peatlands of the Levels, two are of special interest. The Abbot's Way was the first ancient wooden road to be discovered, and its gradual destruction by peat-cutting was a matter of concern to many. The E. J. Godwin (Peat Industries) Ltd. had always assisted our work, and in 1983 the company presented a parcel of land containing about 50 m of the Abbot's Way to the Project. It is now a scheduled Ancient Monument and will eventually pass to the county of Somerset for permanent

plate IX maintenance and protection. We built a replica of the Abbot's Way across the land so visitors can see and walk upon the structure. The adjacent peatland may be cut but is then to be back-filled so the site should have some measure of protection from drying.

The other major structure is the Bronze Age Meare Heath track, discovered long ago and recorded by Arthur Bulleid among others. Most of this is now destroyed, or severely desiccated, but in 1984 a stretch of it, north of the scheduled area, was marked for permanent preservation, and with the benefit of flooding of adjacent cut-out peatland there may be a chance of the track surviving for the future.

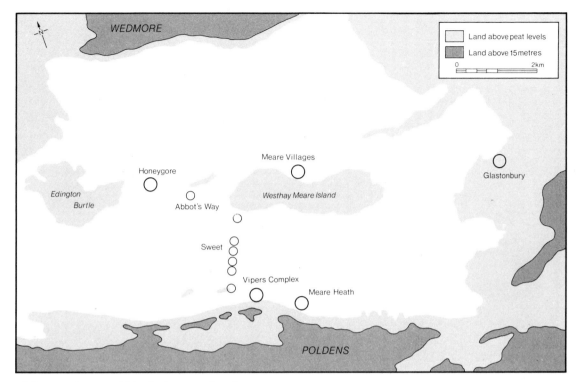

48 Protected areas within the Somerset Levels.

Thus the recognition, acquisition and preservation of parts of the Sweet Track, the Abbot's Way and the Meare Heath track represent an effort on the part of many people and agencies to retain a record of the past. The two Iron Age settlements of Glastonbury and Meare, on pasture land and scheduled as Ancient Monuments, are also assured of protection.

To these structures and sites we can now add several parcels of deep peatland, donated or promised to county agencies by landowners anxious to preserve a part of the natural landscape of the Levels, and one which retains fine records of environmental history as well as supporting varieties of wetland flora and fauna. We also have a large quantity of conserved wooden artifacts numbering in the thousands and either held in museum store for future study or forming segments of rebuilt structures on display in several museums. One problem with wetland archaeology will be apparent, and that is the impermanence of sites. Waterlogged structures cannot be excavated and then left for the public to visit, unlike a stone-built site or an earthwork. The most we can do is to make sure that all interested groups are invited to occasional Open Days, to see a major site at its fleeting exposed best. The visitor who has, so far, travelled farthest to one of our Open Days flew in from Hong Kong, and then flew back! For other people who can come occasionally, or regularly, to

fig. 48

plate 81

191

plate 82   the Levels, our own Somerset Levels Museum, built jointly by the Project and the Willows Peat Company, provides exhibits of conserved wood and other archaeological finds, photographs of our work and of structures now destroyed, and aspects of old peat-cutting techniques. Perhaps encouraged by the displays, visitors may purchase copies of a small booklet, *Prehistory of the Somerset Levels*, which leads to more specific information in our annual *Somerset Levels Papers*, wherein all our surveys, excavations and other studies are reported.

If there is a lesson to be learned from our work in the Levels, it is that the ancient history of a wetland is not immediately visible, and archaeologists must work to demonstrate the presence and importance of such remains. It is only by building up an acceptable body of evidence through publication and other media that the demands for preservation will be made legitimate. Twenty years ago, large areas of the Levels were seasonally inundated permanently wet, with the stratified layers of environmental and human history complete or nearly so. Increased drainage and the demand for peat as fertilizer have now removed much of the record, but cutting of peat created opportunities for our work which we hope to have grasped. Drainage of the land is the great threat now and the future of the Somerset Levels is not in our hands but in the hands of public authorities, and therefore it will be the public at large who will determine what happens next. Only time will tell if the challenge will be met, and if part of this unique landscape will be preserved for the future.

Acknowledgments

Our thanks go to the many people who have contributed to our work in Somerset: the peat-cutters, peat companies and farmers, who have made many of the discoveries, and in particular Sam Foster and the Eclipse Peat Works (Fisons plc), Ricky Rowlands and the E. J. Godwin (Peat Industries) Ltd, and Stan Durston, for long-standing interest and assistance, and Ray Sweet who has the sharpest eyes of anyone on the moors; the Willows Garden Centre for collaboration with us in setting up the Museum of the Somerset Levels; the Willcoxes and Hills of Westhay for providing a base for our diggers and ourselves; the Glastonbury Antiquarian Society and the Somerset Archaeological and Natural History Society for support, in particular Stephen Morland; the Maltwood Fund of the Royal Society of Arts, the Department of the Environment, and the Historic Buildings and Monuments Commission, and the Universities of Cambridge and Exeter for financial and other support over the years, with particular thanks to Geoffrey Wainwright who encouraged us to set up the Project, and Paul Gosling who has helped us in recent efforts to secure parts of the Levels for the future.

The text will reveal our debt to many specialists whose work has complemented the archaeology of the Levels, particularly our environmentalists Alan Hibbert, Stephen Beckett, Maureen Girling and Astrid Caseldine, and Ruth Morgan for tree-ring studies; our combined debt to Arthur Bulleid and Harry Godwin will also be apparent. We particularly thank Sue Rouillard who has produced almost all of the line drawings for this book. Our greatest debt is to the many volunteers who have dug through all weathers, and to our field archaeologists who for almost fifteen years have walked the moors and faced many a hazard in the interests of prehistory.

The quotation at the beginning of chapter 3 is reprinted by permission of Faber and Faber Ltd from *The Complete Poems of Marianne Moore*, 1956.

Bibliography and selected reading

General surveys

COLES, J. M. and ORME, B. J. 1980 *Prehistory of the Somerset Levels*, Somerset Levels Project.
GODWIN, H. 1981 *The Archives of the Peatbogs*, Cambridge University Press.
WILLIAMS, M. 1970 *The Draining of the Somerset Levels*, Cambridge University Press.
ASTON, M. and BURROW, I. 1982 *The Archaeology of Somerset*, Somerset County Council.
BULLEID, A. 1924 *The Lake Villages of Somerset*, Glastonbury Antiquarian Society.

Major reports on prehistoric discoveries

Almost all the work of the Somerset Levels Project has appeared in the annual *Somerset Levels Papers* (abbreviated *Papers* below), starting with volume 1 (1975). The major articles are noted here, first the excavation reports, followed by environmental studies.

The Sweet Track:

COLES, J. M., HIBBERT, F. A. and ORME, B. J. 1973 Prehistoric roads and tracks in Somerset: 3. The Sweet Track, *Proc. Prehist. Soc.* 39, 256–93.
COLES, J. M. and ORME, B. J. 1976 The Sweet Track, Railway Site, *Papers* 2, 34–65.
—— 1979 The Sweet Track: Drove site, *Papers* 5, 43–64.
—— 1981 The Sweet Track 1980, *Papers* 7, 6–12.
—— 1984 Ten excavations along the Sweet Track (3200 bc), *Papers* 10, 5–45.
CASELDINE, A. E. 1984 Palaeobotanical investigations at the Sweet Track, *Papers* 10, 65–78.
GIRLING, M. A. 1979 Fossil insects from the Sweet Track, *Papers* 5, 84–93.
—— 1984 Investigations of a second insect assemblage from the Sweet Track, *Papers* 10, 79–91.
MORGAN, R. A. 1984 Tree-ring studies in the Somerset Levels: the Sweet Track 1979–1982, *Papers* 10, 46–64.

Other Neolithic discoveries and studies:

Walton Heath:
COLES, J. M. and ORME, B. J. 1977a Neolithic hurdles from Walton Heath, Somerset, *Papers* 3, 6–29.
—— 1977b Rowland's hurdle trackway, *Papers* 3, 39–51.
—— 1977c Garvin's Tracks, *Papers* 3, 73–81.
ORME, B. J., CASELDINE, A. E. and MORGAN, R. A. 1982 Recent discoveries on Walton Heath: Garvin's, Bisgrove's and Jones' Tracks, *Papers* 8, 51–64.

ORME, B. J., COLES, J. M., CASELDINE, A. E. and MORGAN, R. A. 1985 Third millennium structures on Walton Heath, *Papers* 11, 62–68.
BECKETT, S. C. 1977 Peat stratigraphy and pollen analysis of the Garvin's Tracks, *Papers* 3, 82–84.
GIRLING, M. A. 1977 Fossil insect assemblages from Rowland's track, *Papers* 3, 51–60.
HIBBERT, F. A. 1977 Peat stratigraphy and pollen analysis from Walton Heath, *Papers* 3, 30–31.
MORGAN, R. A. 1977 Tree-ring studies in the Somerset Levels: the hurdle tracks on Ashcott Heath (Rowland's) and Walton Heath, *Papers* 3, 61–65.
RACKHAM, O. 1977 Neolithic woodland management in the Somerset Levels: Garvin's, Walton Heath and Rowland's tracks, *Papers* 3, 65–71.

Westhay and vicinity:
COLES, J. M. and HIBBERT, F. A. 1968 Prehistoric roads and tracks in Somerset, England: 1. Neolithic. *Proc. Prehist. Soc.* 34, 238–58.
COLES, J. M., HIBBERT, F. A. and CLEMENTS, C. F. 1970 Prehistoric roads and tracks in Somerset, England. 2. Neolithic. *Proc. Prehist. Soc.* 36, 125–51.
COLES, J. M. and HIBBERT, F. A. 1975 The Honeygore Complex, *Papers* 1, 11–19.
COLES, J. M. and ORME, B. J. 1976 The Abbot's Way, *Papers* 2, 7–20.
COLES, J. M. 1980 The Abbot's Way 1979, *Papers* 6, 46–49.
COLES, J. M., FLEMING, A. M. and ORME, B. J. 1980 The Baker Site: a Neolithic platform, *Papers* 6, 6–23.
COLES, J. M., ORME, B. J., CASELDINE, A. E. and MORGAN, R. A. 1985 A Neolithic jigsaw, The Honeygore Complex, *Papers* 11, 51–61.
BECKETT, S. C. and HIBBERT, F. A. 1976 An absolute pollen diagram from the Abbot's Way, *Papers* 2, 24–27.
GIRLING, M. A. 1976 Fossil Coleoptera from the Somerset Levels: The Abbot's Way, *Papers* 2, 28–33.
MORGAN, R. A. 1977 Dendrochronological analysis of the Abbot's Way timbers, *Papers* 2, 21–24.
—— 1980 Tree-ring studies in the Somerset Levels: The Baker site, *Papers* 6, 24–28.
CASELDINE, A. E. 1980 Palaeoenvironmental reconstruction at the Baker site, *Papers* 6, 29–36.

Beaver:
COLES, J. M. and ORME, B. J. 1982 Beaver in the Somerset Levels: some new evidence, *Papers* 8, 67–73.
—— 1983 Homo sapiens or Castor fiber? *Antiquity* 57, 95–102.

Bows:

CLARK, J. G. D. 1963 Neolithic bows from Somerset, England and the prehistory of Archery in northwest Europe, *Proc. Prehist. Soc.* **29**, 50–98.

Pollen zones:

BECKETT, S. C. and HIBBERT, F. A. 1978 The influence of man on the vegetation of the Somerset Levels – a summary, *Papers* **4**, 86–90.
—— 1979 Vegetational change and the influence of prehistoric man in the Somerset Levels, *New Phytol.* **83**, 577–600.

Radiocarbon dates:

ORME, B. J. 1982 The use of radiocarbon dates from the Somerset Levels, *Papers* **8**, 9–25.

Hurdles and woodlands:

ORME, B. J. and COLES, J. M. 1985 Prehistoric woodworking from the Somerset Levels: 2. Species selection and prehistoric woodlands, *Papers* **11**, 7–24.
COLES, J. M. and DARRAH, R. J. 1977 Experimental investigations in hurdle-making, *Papers* **3**, 32–38.
COLES, J. M., ORME, B. J. and HIBBERT, F. A. 1975 The Eclipse Track, *Papers* **1**, 20–24.
COLES, J. M., CASELDINE, A. E. and MORGAN, R. A. 1982 The Eclipse Track 1980, *Papers* **8**, 26–39.
ORME, B. J., STURDY, C. R., and MORGAN, R. A. 1980 East Moors 1979, *Papers* **6**, 52–59.
COLES, J. M. and ORME, B. J. 1978 Structures south of Meare Island, *Papers* **4**, 90–100.
RACKHAM, O. 1980 *Ancient Woodland*, Edward Arnold, London.

Experiments:

COLES, J. M. and DARRAH, R. J. 1977 Experimental investigations in hurdle making, *Papers* **3**, 32–38.
ORME, B. J. and COLES, J. M. 1983 Prehistoric woodworking from the Somerset Levels: 1. Timber, *Papers* **9**, 19–43.
COLES, J. M. and ORME, B. J. 1984 A reconstruction of the Sweet Track, *Papers* **10**, 107–09.
—— 1985 Prehistoric Woodworking from the Somerset Levels: 3. Roundwood, *Papers* **11**, 25–50.

Conservation:

COLES, J. M. and ORME, B. J. 1977 Conservation of Wooden Artifacts from the Somerset Levels: 1, *Papers* **3**, 87–89.
COLES, J. M. 1979 Conservation of Wooden Artifacts from the Somerset Levels: 2, *Papers* **5**, 32–43.
BRYCE, T. 1980 Conservation of the Walton Heath hurdle from the Somerset Levels, *Papers* **6**, 72–75.
COLES, J. M. 1981 Conservation of Wooden Artifacts from the Somerset Levels: 3, *Papers* **7**, 70–78.

Bronze Age discoveries and studies:

Raised bog and flooding horizons:

GODWIN, H. 1981 *The Archives of the Peatbogs*, Cambridge University Press.

BECKETT, S. C. 1978 The environmental setting of the Meare Heath Track, *Papers* **4**, 42–46.
BECKETT, S. C. and HIBBERT, F. A. 1978 The influence of man on the vegetation of the Somerset Levels – a summary, *Papers* **4**, 86–90.
—— 1979 Vegetational change and the influence of prehistoric man in the Somerset Levels, *New Phytol.* **83**, 577–600.

Meare Heath track:

COLES, J. M. and ORME, B. J. 1976 The Meare Heath Trackway: excavation of a Bronze Age Structure in the Somerset Levels, *Proc. Prehist. Soc.* **42**, 293–318.
—— 1978 The Meare Heath Track, *Papers* **4**, 11–39.
BECKETT, S. C. 1978 The environmental setting of the Meare Heath Track, *Papers* **4**, 42–46.
GIRLING, M. A. 1982 The effect of the Meare Heath flooding episodes on the Coleopteran succession, *Papers* **8**, 46–50.
MORGAN, R. A. 1982 Tree-ring studies in the Somerset Levels: the Meare Heath track 1974–1980, *Papers* **8**, 39–45.

Tinney's Ground:

COLES, J. M., ORME, B. J., HIBBERT, F. A. and JONES, R. A. 1975 Tinney's Ground, 1974, *Papers* **1**, 41–53.
COLES, J. M. and ORME, B. J. 1978 Multiple trackways from Tinney's Ground, *Papers* **4**, 47–81.
—— 1980 Tinney's Ground, 1978–1979, *Papers* **6**, 61–68.
MORGAN, R. A. 1980 Tree-ring studies in the Somerset Levels: Tinney's Ground, *Papers* **6**, 69–72.

Other structures and finds:

GODWIN, H. 1960 Prehistoric wooden trackways of the Somerset Levels: their construction, age and relation to climatic change, *Proc. Prehist. Soc.* **26**, 1–36.
DEWAR, H. S. L. and GODWIN, H. 1963 Archaeological discoveries in the raised bogs of the Somerset Levels, England, *Proc. Prehist. Soc.* **29**, 17–49.
COLES, J. M., ORME, B. J., HIBBERT, F. A. and JONES, R. A. 1975 Withy Bed Copse, 1974, *Papers* **1**, 29–38, 40.
COLES, J. M. and ORME, B. J. 1978 Structures south of Meare Island, *Papers* **4**, 90–100.
COLES, J. M., ORME, B. J., CASELDINE, A. E. and MORGAN, R. A. 1985 Godwin's track: a Bronze Age structure at Sharpham, *Papers* **11**, 69–74.
ORME, B. J., COLES, J. M., CASELDINE, A. E. and MORGAN, R. A. 1985 A Later Bronze Age complex at Stileway, *Papers* **11**, 75–79.
COLES, J. M. 1972 Later Bronze Age activity in the Somerset Levels, *Antiquaries Journal* **52**, 269–75.
GIRLING, M. A. 1978 Fossil insect assemblages from Difford's 1 site, *Papers* **4**, 107–13.
—— 1985 An 'old-forest' beetle fauna from a Neolithic and Bronze Age peat deposit at Stileway, *Papers* **11**, 80–83.

Iron Age settlements and studies:

BULLEID, A. and GRAY, H. S. B. 1911, 1917 *The Glastonbury Lake Village*, Glastonbury Antiquarian Society.

—— 1948 *The Meare Lake Village*, vol. 1; Gray and Bulleid 1953, vol. 2; Gray 1966, vol. 3 (ed. M. A. Cotton); Taunton Castle, Taunton.

Re-interpretations:

TRATMAN, E. K. 1970 The Glastonbury lake village: a reconsideration, *Proc. Univ. Bristol Spelaeol. Soc.* 12, 143–67.

CLARKE, D. L. 1972 A Provisional Model of an Iron Age Society and its Settlement System. In D. L. Clarke (ed.) *Models in Archaeology*, 801–70, Methuen, London.

Meare excavations and environments:

ORME, B. J., COLES, J. M. and STURDY, C. R. 1979 Meare Lake Village West: A Report on Recent Work, *Papers* 5, 6–18.

ORME, B. J. COLES, J. M., CASELDINE, A. E. and BAILEY, G. N. 1981 Meare Village West 1979, *Papers* 7, 12–69.

ORME, B. J., COLES, J. M. and SILVESTER, R. J. 1983 Meare Village East 1982, *Papers* 9, 49–74.

GIRLING, M. A. 1979 The fossil insect assemblage from the Meare Lake village, *Papers* 5, 25–32.

Further reports on Meare will be found in *Papers* 12 and 13.

The future

COLES, J. 1984 *The Archaeology of Wetlands*, Edinburgh University Press.

Preservation in the Levels:

COLES, J. M. and ORME, B. J. 1981 The Sweet Track 1980, *Papers* 7, 6–12.

—— 1983 Archaeology in the Somerset Levels 1982, *Papers* 9, 5–6.

Drainage:

WILLIAMS, M. 1970 *The Draining of the Somerset Levels,* Cambridge University Press.

List of illustrations

Unless otherwise credited, photographs are by the authors and drawings by Sue Rouillard.

Colour plates

Monochrome plates

Figures

Index

Figure numbers appear in **bold** and plate numbers in *italic*